MW01234679

STOICISM

The ultimate guide to learn and practice Stoic Philosophy in modern life by dealing with emotion, fear and developing wisdom and calmness to improve yourself daily and lead a good life.

By
Daniel Holiday

Legal & Disclaimer

The information contained in this book and its contents is not designed to replace or take the place of any form of medical or professional advice; and is not meant to replace the need for independent medical, financial, legal or other professional advice or services, as may be required. The content and information in this book have been provided for educational and entertainment purposes only.

The content and information contained in this book have been compiled from sources deemed reliable, and it is accurate to the best of the Author's knowledge, information and belief. However, the Author cannot guarantee its accuracy and validity and cannot be held liable for any errors and/or omissions. Further, changes are periodically made to this book as and when needed. Where appropriate and/or necessary, you must consult a professional (including but not limited to your doctor, attorney, financial advisor or such other professional advisor) before using any of the suggested remedies, techniques, or information in this book.

Upon using the contents and information contained in this book, you agree to hold harmless the Author from and against any damages, costs, and expenses, including any legal fees potentially resulting from the application of any of the information provided by this book. This disclaimer applies to any loss, damages or injury caused by the use and application, whether directly or indirectly, of any advice or information presented, whether for breach of contract, tort, negligence, personal injury, criminal intent, or under any other cause of action.

You agree to accept all risks of using the information presented inside this book.

You agree that by continuing to read this book, where appropriate and/or necessary, you shall consult a professional (including but not limited to your doctor, attorney, or financial advisor or such other advisor as needed) before using any of the suggested remedies, techniques, or information in this book.

Contents

Introduction: The Stoic's First Steps

The term "philosophy" as it was understood in Greco-Roman societies, meant something quite different than what the more modern interpretation typically conveys. At the first mention of philosophy, one's mind perhaps wanders back to that philosophy course they took in college—which incidentally enough, undoubtedly focused heavily on ancient Greek philosophers.

But going back to the source, back to these old-world contemplators themselves, philosophy for them was not just some academic exercise. Philosophy was a means of better understanding the world around them. This is why many of the ancient thinkers, stoic philosophers included, didn't just contemplate better ways to live a virtuous life—but actually lived those lives out. For them it was more than just a thought experiment; it was their everyday existence.

The philosopher at their core, was simply one who was willing to ask a question. Those questions may have been anything from, "Why are we here?" to "Is the Earth flat?" or "What's the best form a society should take?" The philosopher was the tireless inquisitor into all of life's mysteries and speculations. Having that said, Stoicism has been, currently is, and probably always will be a major topic of discussion.

This is because the core tenants of stoicism get to the core tenants of what it means to be a human being. No matter what nation or creed someone may belong to; Stoic philosophy permeates everything we do. Because the fundamental premise of stoicism is to strive to live a virtuous life that has us behaving well toward ourselves and others. Stoicism does not suppress who we are, but rather teaches us how to make the best of our condition.

Stoicism provides us with the ultimate crash course in self-help. For those having a hard time finding their way in life, Stoicism makes the path clear. Quite frankly, the ethics of Stoicism enable you to be—*the best you that you can be.*

Stoicism draws a clear line of distinction between the things we can control and the things we can't. With this clear perspective, Stoics can learn to accept what they can't change while always being mindful of what they can.

There has been a great misunderstanding of stoicism throughout the years. Many are under the false impression that being Stoic means becoming some kind of rationalizing Vulcan (It was good for Mr. Spock, wasn't it?) completely devoid of emotion. And if you were to look in the dictionary and read the definition they have for the word "Stoic," it would only confirm such suspicions.

The actual practice of stoicism however, is not just a cold calculus that resists emotional impulses, but rather a methodology that better teaches one to learn how to channel those impulses as constructively as possible. Stoicism is all about making the best of any given situation. A Stoic does not pine for things they do not have, or fret about things that are out of their control. Yes, the Stoic would indeed try to be calm while in the middle of life's storms (real or metaphorically speaking), but this is not a rejection of emotion.

The Stoic simply realizes that screaming in fear would do absolutely nothing to help the situation. Stoics only respond or act out when they know it will improve their situation, otherwise it's pointless. Just imagine the person stuck in traffic infuriated because another car switched lanes and is now stopped in front of their vehicle.

Honking the horn and screaming isn't going to help the situation. No matter how much the angry motorist honks, that car is still going to be right there, stuck in traffic right along with you.

Honking doesn't do anything at all to improve what just happened, and considering how easily road rage escalates, it would likely only make matters worse. The Stoic, therefore would refuse to lash out or respond, since it would be absolutely pointless to do so. This is perhaps the stereotypical image that many have of a Stoic—an individual calmly dealing with frustrations.

But as mentioned, this side of Stoicism is only in play when it is readily apparent that acting out would do nothing to help the situation. If, however, there are situations in which the Stoic can make real and meaningful change, they will most certainly do it. So, having that said, I would like to personally thank you for purchasing this book because this just might be your first step in a long line of meaningful and virtuous change in your life.

Chapter 1: What is Stoicism? A Brief History

As touched upon in the introduction, Stoicism is a school of thought pertaining to how one should conduct themselves in life. The practice began in approximately 300 BC, under the stewardship of a man simply known as Zeno of Citium. Hailing from Cyprus, Zeno came to Athens as a visitor—according to later accounts he was actually shipwrecked ashore—and in a short time established one of the biggest movements in Greece. Zeno held routine gatherings in front of the famed "Painted Stoa," which in antiquity was basically a portico or "roofed colonnade" where public gatherings were often held.

Here Zeno and his pupils would discuss a wide range of philosophies on life. It was the fact that these devotees met in front of the Painted Stoa, that they would later become known as "Stoics."

Zeno and his Stoics of course were not the only seekers of wisdom on the block, as Athens was at the height of its philosophical prestige at the time. Both Aristotle's Lyceum and Plato's famed Academy for example, were still an integral part of the community. Stoicism was initially just another strand on this great tapestry of intellectual discourse.

The Stoics were just one group among many—and an informal one at that.

Unlike other more established institutions, the Stoics were initially a rag tag bunch without any official organizational structure. It was the power of the message that held them together however, and Zeno had gained a huge following among Greeks by the time of his passing.

Immediately after Zeno's demise a student of his named Cleanthes then took it upon himself to carry on the tradition. Shortly thereafter, Cleanthes was succeeded by another Stoic named Chrysippus. Second to Zeno, Chrysippus would be one of the most influential Stoics of the age, vigorously expanding and expounding upon the foundation that Zeno had laid out.

The next major phase of Stoicism coincided with the rise of Rome. Before the days of Empire, Rome was a Republic. Republican Rome may have been more democratic, but it was still a military power to be reckoned with, whose martial might have been steadily growing while Stoicism was first being developed in Greece. As Rome expanded its influence, many Romans became increasingly interested in the Stoics and their ideals.

Romans quickly found the precepts of Stoicism appealing and would soon seek to make it their own. This would be in large part thanks to the Roman philosopher Cicero who was writing detailed treatise on Stoicism for the Roman public by around mid-1st Century BC. This was followed by other notable Roman philosophers who would carry on the torch of stoicism such as Seneca and Epictetus.

Roman Stoicism would then reach its height in 2nd Century AD under the aegis of none other than the Emperor of Rome himself—Marcus Aurelius, whose book (some call it more of a journal) "Meditations" remains one of the most important works in Stoicism to have ever been written.

Many have noted how intriguing it is that two of the greatest Stoics were Epictetus and Marcus Aurelius. Marcus was the ruler of the most powerful Empire on Earth, while Epictetus was a former slave. To many this is a clear indication the teachings of Stoicism cut across all boundaries and backgrounds; speaking directly to the soul of man.

As Christianity gradually became the official religion of the Roman Empire in the 4th Century under Emperor Constantine, Stoicism as an official movement began to fade. Some would argue however, that many of its principles had found their way into Christianity itself. None other than the Apostle Paul even quotes a Stoic in one of the books of the New Testament.

At any rate, the official practice would be lost until the Renaissance when a revived interest in the classical works of antiquity emerged. Great thinkers such as Descartes, Pascal, and Montaigne began to expound upon the classic Stoic ideals, and apply them to the times in which they lived. The movement has since ebbed and flowed, but has remained as not only a historical lesson, but a valid outlook on life. Here in this book we will explore all of the possibilities that Stoicism might bring.

Chapter 2: The Most Important Figures of Stoic Philosophy

The philosophy of Stoicism did not so much have a founder as it had a whole series of developers. Each of these great thinkers contributed their own unique threads to the rich Stoic tapestry. Let's take a look at each of them, as they are presented here, in more or less chronological order of when they lived and were at their greatest acclaim.

Socrates

Although Socrates predates the founding of official Stoic philosophy, many of the tenants he taught are believed to be forerunners of the practice. Socrates and his Socratic method have many commonalities with what would later become known as Stoicism. Socrates for example, incessantly spoke of the need to think rationally, and use whatever tools one had at their disposal in order to engage in virtuous conduct worthy of a good life.

Socrates furthermore asserted that this goodness was a "virtue" that could be learned with concerted effort. And according to the Socratic method if one learns to question the things around them, even their own behavior, they can give rise to critical thinking that will allow them to discern what is important and what is not important in life.

As testimony of how powerful the Socratic method of reasoning is, this form of rationalization is still being taught in Law Schools, as well as being a prime focus of a lot of Political Science coursework. This methodology is important for these two fields, because it enables one to step outside of their own judgements and opinions, and think critically about the world in which they live.

For a man who is so greatly valued today, it is rather surprising to think of how he was rejected by a large portion of his own contemporary society. He had his own fan base to be sure, but the underlying powers began to plot against him. And as his fame and the popularity of his teachings grew, the authorities in Athens decided to crack down on the philosopher, and had him arrested. On what charges was Socrates arrested? It was claimed that he "refused to acknowledge the gods recognized by the state" and that he was "corrupting the youth."

It seemed that although Socrates had a passionate following among the youth, their parents were none too thrilled. The older "establishment class" as one Bernie Sanders might say, thoroughly rejected what Socrates taught. As is often the case, new revolutionary ideas get pushback from those who fear any change to the status quo. Right or wrong, they saw Socrates and his message as a great disrupter of everything they had come to hold dear.

Socrates was putting all kinds of new-fangled ideas into the minds of their children, and even telling them that reverence for the old gods didn't matter. This was a clear-cut recipe for outrage as far as the elite ruling class of Athens was concerned. They viewed him as a clear and present danger, and decided he must be silenced.

Socrates was hauled into court where it is said a jury of some 500 of his peers had been assembled. After a lengthy trial, Socrates was ultimately found to be guilty as charged and sentenced to death by suicide. It might seem strange to modern readers to sentence someone to suicide, but this was quite common in the ancient world. It was often viewed as both a last-minute mercy, and a means to save the state the trouble of execution, by letting the convicted end their own life.

In later Stoicism suicide was not viewed necessarily as an evil or a bad thing. It was viewed as a possibly rational option if the circumstances merited it. Although a virtuous life would only commit suicide as a last resort, if the Stoic had no better options, suicide was viewed as a valid possibility. Stoics therefore, would not have looked down upon Socrates for acquiescing to the demands of his self-annihilation.

So it was that Socrates was given a cup of poison hemlock to drink.

As he took the cup into his hand, he was calm and resolute. According to Plato's account of the event, Socrates was Stoic until the very end.

Showing no fear in death, he even offered to give those who had condemned him a toast! Nevertheless, when he drank the poison his companions realizing he would soon die were overcome with grief.

Socrates chastised them however, telling them, "You are strange fellows; what is wrong with you? I sent the women away for this very purpose, to stop them from creating such a scene. I have heard that one should die in silence. So please be quiet and keep control of yourselves."

Socrates ultimately died from the poison he was given, his life coming to an end in 399 BC. In the last moments of his life Socrates displayed full reasoned control of his emotions, an example the Stoics would come to emulate in the years to come.

Famed Stoic Epictetus in fact, would highlight Socrates last moments as reason to argue that the fear of death is but a ruse to ensnare the unenlightened.

Epictetus reasoned, "Men are disturbed not by things which happen, but by the opinions about the things. For example, death is nothing terrible, for if it were, it would have seemed so to Socrates; for the opinion about death, that it is terrible, is the terrible thing."

Epictetus argued that death was nothing to fear.

Death was natural and there was nothing particular cruel or evil about it. According to Epictetus and Stoics like him, even the threat of death should not be anything to shake a Stoic from his principles, since even death is but a minor circumstance in the scheme of things.

This is one of the most enlightened realizations any Stoic could come to make, and it was Socrates who first opened their eyes to the possibility.

Socrates may not himself have been a Stoic, but he most certainly lived, and even died, with Stoic principles in mind. As much as Socrates has since been quoted by various schools of thought and philosophy since his death, it is quite astonishing that he himself never wrote anything down in life. We have no direct testimony from Socrate's own pen. Everything we know about him is by way of second or even third hand accounts. Having that said, his virtuous character has served as a great example to the movement all the same.

Zeno of Cyprus

Zeno of Cyprus lived sometime between 340 to 265 BC. He hailed from Cyprus, and came of age at the high point of Alexander the Great. Alexander the Great had cobbled together an Empire that stretched some 3,000 miles, from Macedonia and Greece to Egypt, through the Mideast, across Turkey, over Iran, and pushing all the way to the edge of India.

It was this massive consolidation of land that ushered in what is known as the Hellenistic age.

A time in which ideas and philosophy previously isolated just in Greece, were spread to all the far corners of the Alexander's Empire.

Zeno is said to have arrived in the Greek capital of Athens in 317 BC. It is said that Zeno's arrival was one of calamitous circumstances. His ship had run aground and he had lost almost all of his possessions that were onboard.

Considering the fact Zeno made his living as a trader of goods— most of which were now at the bottom of the sea, this was a devastating loss. Nevertheless, the unfortunate Zeno survived, and made his way ashore. Upon his arrival a depressed, broke, and disillusioned Zeno wandered aimlessly around the streets of Athens. As he ambled about worrying over what his bleak future might hold.

An anecdotal story tells us that Zeno eventually made his way to a local bookstore and became intrigued by the works of philosophy he found there. He was reading through a book about Socrates when he felt compelled to ask the store's owner where he could "find a man like this?"

The Cynic philosopher Crates walked by just at that moment prompting the storekeeper to point at him and proclaim, "Follow him!" And he did. From that point on, Zeno dropped everything and became one of Crate's pupils. Crates taught an aesthetic, monkish lifestyle and was known as one of the so-called "beggar philosophers."

Although Zeno learned much from Crates, he was not destined to be a Cynic, and soon began to formulate philosophical ideas of his own.

And it is said that it was from Crate's cynicism, that Zeno eventually developed what we now know as Stoicism. Zeno also briefly worked under the aegis of a philosopher named Polemo at Plato's famed Academy. But this too was just preparation for Zeno to chart his own philosophical destiny.

It was around 300 BC that Zeno first set off to start his own school of thought. And "school of thought" is a very apt way to describe it, because Zeno and his followers did not meet inside a brick and mortar building. They gathered out in the open sun near a roofed porch, that was known among the locals as the "Stoa Pikile" or roughly translated, the "Painted Colonnade."

This structure was covered with the artistic renderings of several local artists. It was due to this assortment of paintings that covered the colonnade's surface that it was called the "Pained Colonnade," or as it were, the "Stoa Pilie." And it was due to this famous locale that those who regularly gathered there, began to be referred to as "Stoics."

Much of Zeno's written work has been lost, but from the bits and pieces that have survived, we have an interesting picture of who this man was and what he taught. It was of course, Zeno who identified "Logos" or "Universal Reason" as the great source of the "ultimate good in life."

Zeno put so much stock in reason, that he believed if the populace was properly instructed, there would be no need for laws, since the enlightened man would be reasonable enough to live in peace.

According to Zeno, by contrast, those who did not practice a life of reason and logic were nothing more than a beast inflamed by uncontrollable passion.

A dog after all, is not able to ponder its existence. When was the last time you heard of a dog asking the question; why are we here? What's the point of this existence? Is there life after death? You are not likely to hear your beloved little pooch pondering such things on your next dog walk, that's for sure. So it was that the Stoics intuitively knew that it was man who was uniquely positioned to utilize the reason he had been endowed with to sort out the ultimate questions in life.

Zeno was not out to start a religion, revolution, or anything else so grandiose, he was merely seeking to ask questions. It was this spirit of debate that permeated the gatherings at the Stoa Pilie. The Stoics, who came from all classes and backgrounds were equal searchers for truth. In many ways what Zeno started was antiquity's version of the think tank group, seeking to find the best way to approach their lives.

Aratus of Soli

Aratus of Soli is perhaps a lesser known figure of stoicism but he is still important all the same. He came from Soli, a region located in today's modern Turkey. Aratus came to Athens as a youth just as Stoicism was gaining traction, and quickly became an authority on the subject. Around 276 BC he traveled to Macedon where he was given a position with the court of King Antigonus Gonatus. It is interesting to note, that Zeno himself, the founder of Stoicism, had rejected just such a role.

At any rate, as evidence of how respected a courtier Aratus of Soli must have been, he was later sent to Syria to work for Antiochus I, one of the great Hellenistic rulers of the day. Antiochus was said to have been a "patron of the arts."

The king had just pacified one of his greatest regional antagonists—the Gauls, and was now interested in bringing knowledgeable and talented men to serve in his administration during the ensuing peace.

Aratus certainly fit that bill. But beyond his resume as court minister, he is perhaps best known for his poetry. Although most of the primary manuscripts have been lost, his work is widely quoted by his contemporaries. The poems of Aratus extoled Stoic virtues and were so memorable, that even the Apostle Paul knew enough to mention them when he sought to convert the Greek masses to Christianity during his visit to Athens around 51 AD.

Paul had preached to those assembled, "Yet he [God] is actually not far from each of us, for 'In him we live and move and have our being;' as even some of your own poets have said, 'For we are indeed his offspring.'"

That poet whom Paul so famously quoted, was in fact Aratus of Soli the Stoic who reasoned that we are indeed, all children of God. The exact words the Apostle Paul is quoting from can be found in this Stoic philosopher's seminal work, which was called "Phaenomena."

It was a complex work in which Aratas spoke at length about everything from constellations to the weather, as well as setting down lines of lyrical prose about the nature of divinity. It is said that Phaenomena in some sense, presents itself almost like an ancient version of a "farmer's almanac," instructing the laity about the nature of the changes of the seasons.

Yet within these mundane observations are his insightful flourishes about the nature of God and how we are his offspring whom he has given these "natural signs" as a helpful to "conduct our business." At any rate Phaenomena was no doubt this Stoic's masterpiece. And with his life's work complete, Aratus is believed to have passed away sometime around 240 BC.

Aristo of Chios

Aristo was yet another student of Zeno. He was a firm believer in the teaching of Stoic ethics. Aristo further made the claim that the sole virtue worth pursuing was a "healthy state of mind."

One of Aristo's chief arguments and contributions to stoicism was the idea that not all supposed "morally indifferent" instances in life, necessarily have "precedence."

What does this mean? It means that there are circumstances in life in which one may prefer something that is normally a negative experience if the conditions required it.

If for example, someone has become enslaved by a wicked ruler who forces the healthy to work, it just might become more expedient for that person to become sick so they would be left alone.

Aristo discovered and pointed out there were many grey areas in this Stoic line of thought. He essentially rejected the idea that there was always a moral certainty as it pertained to certain situations in life. In some cases, things were just too ambiguous to quantify them as being either completely good or completely bad.

As simple as the concept might sound to us today, such thinking was revolutionary in the ancient world. Since in those days almost every action had long been ascribed to have great meaning behind it. If someone became terribly sick out of nowhere for example, the prevailing belief might have been that the sick person was being somehow judged by divine forces.

For the ancients, they didn't see it as an indifferent matter at all. If their neighbor came down with the flu, they just might think they did something to deserve it. This sort of thinking would be considered absurd today, but it was quite common back then. Aristo was one however, who rationalized that such things could be neither good nor evil, as it pertains to both their origin and their repercussions.

Sphaerus

Sphaerus, an ardent follower of Zeno, taught extensively in Sparta, as well as being a frequent fixture at the Egyptian court of Ptolemy IV, who reigned over a successor kingdom that was once part of Alexander the Great's Empire. In King Ptolemy's court. Sphaerus is said to have held impassioned debates on Stoic ideals. And in one such instance he spoke at length on the Stoic virtue of wisdom.

During the course of this discussion, he was asked at one point whether or not a wise man would also be a highly opinionated man. Sphaerus steadfastly insisted that this would not be the case. He declared that being opinionated did not make one wise. Opinions, after all could just be false impressions.

King Ptolemy then wishing to test the wisdom of Sphaerus had a servant bring him a platter of fake, "wax pomegranates" to see if Sphaerus could be tricked into trying to eat them. Sphaerus fell for the trick and tried to bite into the fake fruit.

The King was apparently delighted that Sphaerus fell for the ruse, and proceeded to ridicule him for unwittingly falling prey to a "false impression." Sphaerus was ready with a rebuttal of his own however, as he informed the king that his "assent was not to the impression" that the fake fruit was real, but rather "to the impression it was reasonable" to believe they were.

In other words, he had no reason to believe the wax fruits were fake, so it wasn't an unwise choice to make after all. Sphaerus showed it wasn't so much the results of our choices that made us wise, but the intentions we had in the first place. The result of Sphaerus's choice to try and eat a piece of fake, wax fruit, was not wise in itself. But the fact he assumed there was no reason for King Ptolemy to feed him fake food, was reasonable enough. Although a supposed guest of the king, Sphaerus's time at Ptolemy's court appears to have been an anxious one, in which both the king and his ministers repeatedly tested him. As was the case on yet another occasion when a member of the king's inner circle, a man named Mnesistratus actually accused the Stoic of failing to recognize Ptolemy's authority as king.

The reason for this charge?

Mnesistratus had been apparently paying attention to Sphaerus's lectures on philosophy and had picked up on the fact that it was part of Sphaerus's belief that only one who is "wise and philanthropic" may be called king.

It remains unclear why Mnesistratus felt that Sphaerus was insinuating that King Ptolemy wasn't "wise and philanthropic" enough, but he ended up suggesting Sphaerus was somehow slighting the king.

This was a very serious charge, since Ptolemy no doubt, would have had men killed for far lesser offences. Sphaerus had a simple answer to the charges however, by responding, "Such being Ptolemy, he is king as well." The answer sounds vague enough, but what Sphaerus was suggesting was that Ptolemy IV—who came from a long line of Ptolemaic kings— certainly had the capacity to be king if he so chose, even if he wasn't quite living up to that standard at the moment.

The answer he gave was apparently sufficient, and Sphaerus was allowed to continue his tenure in peace. As such clever insight might indicate, Sphaerus was indeed a wise Stoic, and thanks to his tireless efforts he was instrumental in spreading Stoicism far and wide.

Cleanthes

Cleanthes, arrived on the philosophical scene in Athens, from the town of Assos, situated about 30 miles away from Troy, in what is today modern Turkey.

Cleanthes began his life's work from a rather humble position. During the evenings, he worked as a "drawer of water" to earn a living, while during the day he spent all of his free time studying philosophy.

Demonstrating his fortitude, Cleanthes essentially worked his way through school.

First, he studied under Zeno's former teacher Crates the Cynic, but soon thereafter he shifted gears and began to actively study Stoicism. This devotion quickly earned him Zeno's esteem and he was soon considered a direct successor of the cause of Stoicism. Cleanthes emerged as a Stoic leader in 263 BC and would remain at the helm for about 32 years. Cleanthes lived to an advanced age, reaching about 99 years of age before he passed away.

During the course of his long life, his most famous written work was the "Hymn to Zeus" which was a combination of philosophical and religious themes. Most memorable in the text was the argument Cleanthes made that evil in the world was not the result of an evil creator (God) but due to the evil of man and his decisions.

Yet curiously enough, Cleanthes was also a big believer in fate. In his "Hymn to Zeus" he declared that "fate guides the willing, but drags the unwilling."

Such beliefs seem to present a bit of a paradox, suggesting that one could believe in free will and man's propensity for making evil decisions, and yet at the same time everything is preordained by fate.

Cleanthes was perhaps most famous however, for arguing that once someone obtained virtue it could not be lost.

This belief was directly disputed by fellow philosopher Chrysippus however, who insisted there were indeed mitigating circumstances that could cause someone to lose the virtue they have gained.

Chrysippus

Chrysippus, yet another arrival from Turkey, hailed from Cilicia. Chrysippus took a lead role in Stoicism in 232 BC. He was an important successor of Zeno who greatly reworked many of Zeno's philosophies to his own end. It is Chrysippus who is largely viewed as mainstreaming stoicism for the masses, in his own orthodox version. Among the tenants of this orthodoxy that Chrysippus espoused, was the stoic notion of "Conflagration."

Which is a philosophy that the universe came into being in a great fiery conflagration, only to die, first becoming "air" and then transforming into "water" before a "remnant" of debris circulated and formed "new worlds."

The Stoics believed this was a process that repeated several times. The interesting thing about all this, is the fact that it matches up with some ideas in modern physics as to how the universe may have actually begun.

Some scientists who subscribe to string theory have come up with a notion of how the universe came about, which they call the "ekpyrotic universe." In this theory the universe cycles from heat to water to solid in much the same way as Chrysippus described. The idea that a man from ancient Greece would come up with a notion similar to one found in the modern concept of string theory, is incredible to say the least.

Along with contemplating the origin of the universe, Chrysippus also focused on much more down to earth matters. And as much as he revised certain aspects of Zeno's teaching, Chrysippus was noted for his defense of one of Zeno's most controversial concepts—his so-called "community of wives."

Zeno had taught that "any man should lie with any woman." In other words, he supported a kind of free love society. The most immediate rebuke of such a notion was usually in regard to who would raise the offspring of all these wild unions. According to Chrysippus the solution to this would be to have all children raised by the "elders" of society.

But perhaps most famously, it was Chrysippus who maintained that virtue once gained could be lost in the case of "intoxication or madness."

This was a point that he took up with Cleanthes, who insisted that virtue in the end, could not just suddenly slip through a Stoic's fingers. Chrysippus saw things differently however, and felt that virtue was not a given. According to Cleanthes, virtue not only had to be gained, but it also had to be cultivated and maintained.

Antipater of Tarsus

It is generally believed that Antipater of Tarsus was an important figure in the Stoic movement, and yet through the sands of time, very little information is readily available on him. It is from Plutarch, that we get a sense of his greatness, since this ancient historian identifies Antipater as being on the same level as Zeno, Cleanthes, and Chrysippus.

Antipater was not much of a reformer, as he was an advocator. As such, it is said that he did not create too many of his own "innovations" he mostly just advocated tenants that were already in place. The main thing that is known about Antipater's teaching, is his views on God. Unlike other Stoics who stayed away from the personification of deity, Antipater laid out his beliefs that the supreme being was "blessed, incorruptible, and of good will to men."

He also delved into the supernatural through his studies in divination and precognition.

In this sense, this Stoic seemed to bridge the gap between paranormal belief and every day practice. Antipater truly ran the philosophical gamut, but most of the information on what Antipater wrote and taught however, comes to us secondhand, since the original works have been lost.

Panaetius of Rhodes

Panaetius was a student of Antipater of Tarsus. Panaetius was from a well-off family and could have no doubt led a successful life outside of philosophy, but instead chose to study with the great thinkers of Greece. After cutting his philosophic teeth in Athens, Panaetius went off to Rome. It was here, among the Romans that he would gain a great following for Stoicism.

And it was one prominent Roman in particular, Scipio Aemilianus, that Panaetius managed to galvanize to the Stoic ideal early on. Scipio wishing to spread the knowledge he gained from Panaetius would then go on to form the so-called Scipionic Circle, in which several up and coming teachers, philosophers, politicians, and poets would meet to debate a wide range of topics, with Stoicism often being one of them.

It was after Scipio passed away in 129 BC that Panaetius decided to go back to Greece.

Panaetius himself is most remembered for taking the mystery out of Stoicism for the common people.

Panaetius though from a prominent background himself, had an affinity for the common man and was quite good at explaining Stoic ideas in a way that everyone could understand, so that they could apply the concepts to their own individual lives.

Among other things, Panaetius often spoke of how man's most "valuable possession" was the ability to reason. Panaetius argued that by contrast, animals are governed by impulses that default for self-preservation. According to Panaetius, man's ultimate driving force is reason. It was the contention of Panaetius that it was this innate ability to reason that enabled human beings to cooperate with each other on a larger scale.

Panaetius also contended there is no one size fits all philosophy. In the past, Stoics looked toward a wise sage to emulate, such as Socrates or Zeno, but Panaetius stressed that the goal is not to become someone else, but rather for each to search out "their own ideal, suited to their capacity."

In comparison to predecessors such as Antipater and Chrysippus, Panaetius is considered a middle of the road type of Stoic leader, with a more moderate approach to Stoicism than some of the purists who came before. Where Antipater would firmly stand by long held doctrine of the Stoic movement, Panaetius wasn't afraid to chart his own course.

And in doing so, Panaetius created a more practical and pragmatic brand of Stoic teachings that could be more readily applied for everyday life.

It is for this reason therefore that the epoch of moderate Stoicism over which Panaetius presided was called "Middle Stoicism."

Dardanus

Dardanus a native of Athens, was another notable student of Antipater of Tarsus, and an eventual successor of Panaetius. After Panaetius died in 109 BC, the Athenian school began to split into various sects and Dardanus was one of the main leaders. It was a new and exciting phase of Stoic thought, with many diverging viewpoints that had emerged and Dardanus played a pivotal role.

Unfortunately, however, not much else is known of this Stoic, since much of the original texts have been lost. And it is believed that by the time Cicero, the great Roman Stoic, emerged on the scene around 79 BC, Dardanus had already passed on. With a lack of historic record intact, from the few sparse outside references available, we can only surmise about the legacy he left to those who came after him.

Quintus Lucilius Balbus

One leading Stoic that the great Cicero must indeed have run into during his younger days in Athens was Quintus Lucilius Balbus. We know this because Cicero would write about him quite extensively.

But perhaps most famously was the piece Cicero wrote called, "On the Nature of the Gods" in which he used Balbus as an effective plot device in his dialogue.

In this epic, along with Quintus being employed by Cicero to speak for Stoicism, he also made use of the Epicurean philosopher Gaius Velleius and the skeptic, Gaius Cotta. Cicero has each one of them present their views throughout the course of the text. It is of course a fictional narrative, written to make a point, but the way it presents these characters bouncing philosophical ideas off of each other is eye opening all the same. In addition to this mention, Quintus also makes an appearance in Cicero's "Hortensius," which debates the best way for one to spend their "leisure time." Cicero's answer? Studying philosophy of course. And the Stoic Quintus Lucilius Balbus would most likely have agreed.

Cato the Younger

His full name is Marcus Porcius Cato Uticensis, but he is much better known as simply "Cato the Younger." Cato isn't known so much for any great works he penned on Stoicism, but rather for his efforts as an unceasing promoter of the cause.

Cato was a Roman and in the last days of the Roman Republic he ceaselessly spread the ideals of Stoic philosophy far and wide.

He was also one who practiced what he preached and became a prime example—even a mentor, of what a Stoic life should truly be all about. If Cato was sick or in pain for example, he was known to simply grin and bear it just as Stoic doctrine advised. Cato had developed a phenomenal self-control that enabled him to endure hardship without complaint.

He was also a great advocate of Stoic ascetism, and even though he had the resources to buy good food, fine wine, and nice clothes, he often deprived himself, and did without. Cato found value in the simple things in life and didn't need to surround himself with the trapping of wealth in order to feel fulfilled.

One of the most profound moments of Cato displaying his Stoic virtue however, came about when he was attacked by a man in one of the local bathhouses that were so common in Rome at the time. Romans of all stripes would relax in the community bathhouses. They were meant to be a refuge and safe haven for all.

But Cato was savagely attacked by a belligerent assailant while visiting one of these facilities. The next day the man apparently had remorse for what he had done however, and approached Cato to apologize. Cato, showing his Stoic capacity to forgive and forget, quite literally told the man, "I don't even remember being hit."

As usual, Cato served as a living example of the Stoic ideal.

Sadly, this stoic role model's time would come to a close, when Julius Caesar rose to power. Cato knowing that the Roman Republic was at an end, decided to take his own life. He committed suicide by his own sword in 46 BC.

Marcus Tullius Cicero

Cicero—his name sounds familiar to many of us. There are streets named after him and even whole towns can be found, that bear his appellation; scattered all across the globe. But who was he? Cicero was a prominent politician and philosopher who lived near the end of the era of the Roman Republic. Along with engaging in philosophy, Cicero was a man who wore many hats. At various times he was also an attorney, praetor, and consul. Along with all of these roles, whether or not Cicero was also a true Stoic, is a matter which is still debated.

Cicero after all, was well versed in many schools of philosophical thought, and he was not necessarily solely partial just to the ideals of Stoicism alone.

But at any rate, he was most certainly influenced by Stoics, holding Stoic philosophical teachings in high regard, and amending them with his own thoughts wherever he could.

Though Cicero occasionally differed with mainstream Stoic doctrine, on most of the core tenants of Stoic ethics, he was in direct alignment.

And as such his commentary on Stoicism is considered quite useful, even if whether he can be considered a pure Stoic or not, remains in question.

At any rate, for anyone studying Stoicism, Cicero is inescapable. Cicero's words can be found right at the heart of stoic discourse. His soaring rhetoric would only come to an end when he was executed in 43 BC after his failed attempts of preserving the Roman Republic came to naught.

Porcia Catonis

Porcia Catonis was the daughter of Cato the Younger. Following in the footsteps of her father Cato, she grew up to blaze her own rich and unique path as a Stoic.

She also just so happened to be the wife of the infamous "Brutus" who took part in the "Ides of March" assassination of Julius Caesar. Brutus was the one whose name was allegedly invoked in the dying words of Caesar. Stabbed and bloodied, Caesar allegedly looked up at Brutus and gasped in disbelief, "You too Brutus?"

One of the more interesting tales, as it pertains to Porcia relates to this infamous event. It is said that when Brutus and the other conspirators were plotting to overthrow Caesar's dictatorship, Porcia although left out of the loop, sensed her husband was hiding something from her. She then confronted him about it, but he still refused to divulge any information.

It was then when Porcia determined her husband was not being discreet with her because "she was a woman." She believed Brutus was concealing his secret from her because he was under the belief she might crack, and tell all under pressure. As such, she sought to prove Brutus otherwise. She wanted to prove to him that she could be just as strong and resilient as anyone else. In her efforts to do so, she supposedly stabbed herself in the thigh with a knife. It is said she then used Stoic principles to ignore the terrible pain for an entire day. She quite literally suffered in silence, not telling her husband, not crying out, and not saying a word. This is some serious Stoic resilience to say the least.

The next day she then showed the terrible wound to her husband and declared it as proof of her ability to be able to keep his confidence. This was apparently enough to have Brutus convinced, and he thereafter let her in on the plot. Of course, it remains unclear whether this story ever actually happened in the first place. If it's true, it would also seem sadly ironic that the daughter of Cato the Younger, a man who had stabbed himself with his own sword, would in turn stab herself with a knife.

At any rate, true or not, the mere fact that the chroniclers deemed it worthwhile to mention this female Stoic shows how important she was to the movement.

And for a woman to even be considered as an equal in such pursuits in the ancient world, which typically relegated women to background roles, is demonstrative of how progressive the Stoics really were.

Attalus

Attalus lived during the time of Christ, and was most active after 20 AD. Attalus began his journey to Stoicism after he hit hard times financially.

He lost the once extensive land holdings he had and was forced to "cultivate the ground" just to earn a meagre subsistence.

It was during this time of hardship that Attalus embraced Stoicism. It seems he was a man who hit rock bottom and Stoicism provided a way for him to cope with the dire straits he had found himself in.

Beyond these basic anecdotes however, not much more about his life or works have survived the ravages of time. In the end, he is largely remembered due to his star pupil and later Stoic— Lucius Annaeus Seneca who would become one of the greatest influences on Stoicism of all time.

Seneca for one, forever cherished the days he spent with Attalus and later described himself as having, "practically laid siege to his classroom first to arrive and last to leave." Even though much of Attalus's original works are lost, his character and example still shine forth all the same.

Lucius Annaeus Seneca

Sometimes referred to as "Seneca the Younger" and other times just "Seneca"—whatever you call him, he was a force to be reckoned with. Living out most of his life in 1st Century AD— since the days of his youth, Seneca soaked up all of the current of philosophy that flowed through the Greco-Roman world. Seneca learned to deal with hardship and reversals early on in life.

One of which occurred in 41 AD when the Roman Emperor, Claudius, had Seneca exiled to the island of Corsica. It had been alleged he had committed adultery with the Emperor's sister. And while it has never been determined whether the charges were true or not, the mere accusation was enough to ruin what had otherwise been a promising career.

True to the tenants of Stoicism however, Seneca didn't complain. He put on a brave face, and determined to make the best of his new home in exile. During his time on Corsica he wrote letters to friends and family, composed poetry, and even studied geography, taking advantage of the unique layout of the island.

Seneca was ultimately returned from exile in 49 AD, and due to his good behavior was deemed suitable as a tutor for the soon-to-be Emperor, Nero. It was when Nero came to power in 54 AD that Seneca was made a top advisor of the Roman court. For the first few years Seneca was an invaluable member of Nero's inner circle and was treated with great respect.

Seneca would eventually face another sudden reversal however and fall out of favor with Nero.

Such things were not too hard to do when employed by such a tyrant, but the results were devastating for Seneca all the same.

Nero had made Seneca prosperous as his valued advisor, but once the Emperor began to suspect Seneca's allegiance was faltering, he was more than ready to dispatch with him, and in 65 AD, after Seneca was accused of plotting against the Emperor, he was ordered to commit suicide—which he stoically did.

In life and in death, Seneca has been portrayed as the perfect example of how a Stoic should accept external factors beyond their control. One of course, might argue that Seneca could have refused to take his own life, he could have fought back. But Seneca was an old man at this point, and he knew that if he didn't comply, Roman soldiers would be sent in to finish him off anyway.

At any rate, Seneca's example during his last days is generally viewed as a positive for Stoicism, as it displayed the Stoic virtue of standing firm in the face of death.

His written work meanwhile which consists of several plays, prose and essays, continues to speak to us long after his demise.

Epictetus

Proving that Stoicism knew no bounds, Epictetus is one of the greatest of Stoics, yet began from the humblest of beginnings. He was a slave at Nero's court as a young man but was freed upon Nero's death in 68 AD.

Upon gaining his freedom he became an expert on Stoicism and began to actively teach Stoic principles.

He was known as being a passionate and powerful speaker who insisted on the Stoic principle that one should not go against the flow of external events but instead stoically accept them for what they are. Or as Epictetus himself would put it, "Do not try to make what happens happen as you wish, but wish for what happens in the way it happens and then the current of your life will flow easily."

Epictetus consistently preached this message to whoever would listen. His discourse would be interrupted in 92 AD however, when Emperor Domitian decided to order a wholesale banishment of all philosophical speakers from the Roman capital. After being denied access to Rome, Epictetus settled in the city of Nicopolis where he continued to deliver his message until his death in 135 AD.

Although Epictetus himself, never wrote anything down, a student of his named "Arrian" transcribed many of his lectures. These transcriptions would end up published as the masterpiece works, "Discourses" and the "Enchiridion."

A main theme carried throughout Epictetus's work, is the Stoic idea that we shouldn't worry so much about changing external circumstances since it is the divine will, that sets everything into motion.

Marcus Aurelius

Marcus Aurelius, a man who was destined to become the Emperor of the world's greatest Empire, was schooled in Stoicism at an early age. Even as he was being groomed to take the place of the previous Emperor, Antonius Pius, Marcus was knee deep in works of Stoic wisdom.

Marcus ultimately became Emperor in 161 AD and his reign would span nearly 20 years, only coming to an end when he died in 180 AD. He is known as being one of the last so-called "Good Emperors" and is noted for his compassion, and leniency toward his subjects. Marcus was allegedly so humane that he ordered the popular gladiator games to be waged with blunted weapons so no one could stab anybody.

But what has stood the test of time the most with this Stoic philosopher was his work, "Meditations" in which he compiled several thought-provoking essays on what it meant to be a Stoic. His philosophical feelings have gained a great resurgence in recent years, and has become especially pertinent to the Modern Stoicism movement of today.

This is quite extraordinary considering the fact that Marcus Aurelius never actually intended for his journal to be published!

Marcus was one who greatly admired the work of Epictetus. He often embraced the Stoic ideal that man's efforts are insignificant in the grand scheme of fate. And just like Epictetus he sought to live a life that went with the flow of destiny, rather than against it. The fact an Emperor was such an avid admirer of the teachings of Epictetus, a man who was a former slave, is evidence of just how transcending and far reaching the teachings of Stoicism really were.

Chapter 3: Stoic Views on Logos, Consciousness, and the Soul

Before diving into the practical Stoic principles that can be applied to everyday life, let's take a look at the larger view that the Stoics took of Logos (divine will), consciousness, and the soul. For some it was a matter of religion, for others it was simply how they perceived the universe. Often enough the views converged, briefly broke off, and then came back full circle again. Putting it all together—here is how the Stoics perceived their world.

The Concept of Logos

The most encompassing school of thought in Stoicism is that of what they referred to as "logic." This area of intellectual debate sought to understand the underpinnings of man's ability to reason as well as the "logos" which roughly translates as "word" behind it. But for the ancient Greeks, logos meant more than these simple translations might convey. Logos essentially meant the divine word/reason that permeates throughout the universe.

Logos was nothing short of the very consciousness of the universe itself. But the Greeks also used logos in reference to more mundane rhetoric, so in a sense the word had a double meaning depending on the context in which it was used. Interestingly enough, one of the most famous verses of the Christian Bible seems to borrow from this Greek concept of logos, and in at least this instance of usage, the reference to divine reason cannot be mistaken.

Because as the first few verses of the Book of John proclaim, "In the beginning was the Word, and the Word was with God, and the Word was God." This is of course the traditional English translation. In the original Greek that the New Testament was written in however, instead of "Word" the text would read, "Logos." So, if you will pardon my mixture of Greek and English, let's take that same text and swap "Word" for "Logos." It would then read, "In the beginning was the Logos, and the Logos was with God, and the Logos was God."

For a Greek speaking audience, especially one from the 1st Century when the text was written, the meaning would have been unmistakable. The New Testament was echoing the idea of a divine will/consciousness permeating the universe. Of course, the Christian text would go on to say that the Logos had manifested on Earth in the flesh, in the form of Jesus Christ. As the Book of John states, "And the Logos became flesh and dwelt among us."

Many Greeks would indeed later become Christians, but even those who didn't accept the manifestation of Christ, would have recognized the concept of a divine consciousness permeating all of creation, just as their own philosophers had spoken of. Nevertheless, speaking of such comparisons presents difficulties to the beliefs of both mainstream Stoics and Christians since the interpretation seems to border dangerously close to Pantheism.

Pantheists believe that everything in the universe is a manifestation of God—that we are all literally pieces of God manifesting in this plane of existence, whether we realize it or not. And although the likes of the Apostle Paul and the Stoic Aratus—whom Paul once quoted at length on this subject—no doubt both agreed that we are the "children of God," neither one would have gone so far as to say that we are literally *part of God*. This would have been taking things a bit too far for both schools of thought.

Stoic Takes on Free Will and the Nature of Evil

No matter what the religion, spiritual movement, or school of philosophical thought, the idea of evil has always been a hotly debated issue. If one believes in a divine will that permeates the universe, just how does this divine will square with all of the evil in the world? For early Christians the answer was the free will of sinful man. Consequentially enough, this is yet another direct parallel with Stoicism. Because Cleanthes proclaimed much the same thing, except of course the god he referred to was named "Zeus."

It was in Cleanthes's "Hymn to Zeus" that had him insisting divine will did not ordain anything evil, and all things bad were simply the result of "bad men." According to Cleanthes, "the bad man appears as an independent originator of some happenings which God, who had no hand in devising them, is clever enough to turn to serve his purposes."

In some ways this argument seems to actually refute the concept of free will, since Cleanthes is basically saying that in some cases human beings think they our plotting their own course—albeit a bad one—when in reality they are being manipulated to serve the greater purpose of divinity. In other words, even when man thinks he is exerting his own willpower it is God who has the final say in the long run.

Chrysippus had an even bleaker view on free will, and basically rejected it outright. He instead believed in fate—he believed that our destinies were written before we were born and we were simply acting out the roles we were given by the divine will of the universe. Strangely enough however, even though Chrysippus laid out his belief that our roles are predetermined. He still insisted that virtuous acts committed by individuals should be praised, and bad acts should be condemned.

It doesn't seem to make much sense to blame someone for things that—according to his view—were preordained to begin with. It was the contradictory nature of this belief that gave way to the so-called "Argument of Inaction" which asked the question why we should act at all, if our course was already charted. Here it was understandably argued, "why we should give people advice, reproof, exhortation and punishment, if their actions were pre-determined." In other words—why should we do anything at all? If fate has already decided the outcome, why should we bother?

But perhaps even more glaring than the Argument of Inaction, when it comes to this take on fate, was the idea that the divine will had preordained all manner of evil acts. This would be a seeming contradiction in the belief of a divine and benevolent will at work in the universe. But Chrysippus stuck to his argument, and found his own solution to the dilemma.

Chrysippus theorized that evil existed merely as a consequence of good. He reasoned that without evil to contrast goodness with, there would be no way to conceptualize good in the first place. Just like you need hunger to understand satiated, you need evil to understand good. It is a shockingly simple, yet highly effective argument. According to Chrysippus, without evil, there would be no good. They are polar opposites, but they coexist together. According to this Stoic belief, quite frankly, one could not exist without the other.

Stoic Views on the Soul

The Stoics had wide ranging views on the soul and most especially what might happen to the soul after the shedding of the physical form. Some believed that shortly after death the soul dissipated like a fine mist, and went back to the universe from whence it had come. This view held that after death the soul ceased to be an individual—putting an end to the individual and separate life as we knew it on Earth.

Others, however believed the soul as an intact form of our consciousness that would go on after death. For the ancient Greeks, the concept of soul translated into a world familiar to modern psychology as "psyche." For the Stoic—regardless of what they believed happened to the psyche upon death, they viewed it as the causative factor of living, from which all perception and emotion emerged.

In other words, the psyche was the seat of consciousness. With this concept established, it was then wondered if the universe as a whole had a seat of consciousness. Some argued that even the Earth was a living being with its own "world soul." Cleanthes famously picked up this argument, and proceeded to logically expound upon the idea there must be a hierarchy of consciousness all throughout the universe.

Cleanthes described, "If one nature is better than another, there must be a nature that is best. If one soul is better than another, there must be a soul that is best. And if one living thing is better than another, there must be a living thing who is best. In such cases there is no run to infinity. So, there is no infinite progression of living things, any more than there is of natures or souls. But clearly one living thing is better than another, as a horse is better than a tortoise and a bull than a donkey and a lion than a bull... What is perfect and best would be superior to man, replete with all the virtues and untouched by any ill. This will be identical with God. Therefore, there is a God."

Chapter 4: What are the Ethics of Stoicism?

The centerpiece of stoic philosophy is their understanding of ethics. According to the Stoic, anything which was virtuous or "morally perfect" in nature, was to be set apart from all other things. For them living a good life was living a life of virtue. For the Stoic "good" was an "absolute term" designated only for things that were truly virtuous in nature and incorruptible.

People might, for example think having a lot of money was a good thing, but money is corruptible and could be used for nefarious purposes; so, money in itself therefore could not be quantified as good. The only things truly good according to the ethics of stoicism were things that could not be used for illicit purposes. Stoics further believed the only way someone could be a virtuous person was if they had the wisdom to know what was virtuous in the first place.

It was believed that a virtuous man by nature would also have to be a knowledgeable man—one who searched for the bigger meaning in life. In other words; a philosopher.

It was the pursuit of higher knowledge that allowed someone to gain virtue.

It was in this area where the stoic Chrysippus, came into a dispute with Cleanthes, over whether or not virtue could be lost once it was attained.

Chrysippus argued that it was indeed possible, laying out hypothetical situations in which someone might literally lose their mind, suffer a psychological breakdown, and deviate from the path of virtue.

Cleanthes didn't see it that way however, and argued that once virtue was gained it could not be lost. Curiously, this debate seems to almost echo later arguments of Christians when it came to salvation. Christians of course, believe they have salvation through placing faith in Christ, as well as doing their best to live a virtuous life. Almost since the beginning of Christianity however, Christian believers have debated about what would happen if someone fell away from Christ. Would they lose their salvation? Or as a stoic would put it—would they lose their virtue?

Chrysippus believed that something gained could indeed be lost, but Cleanthes on the other hand echoed the Christian equivalent of "once saved, always saved" by steadfastly proclaiming that once one gained virtue it could not be lost. But all of this called into question the role of human will. Virtue and wisdom did not stand alone in what was needed for a good life, the philosophers argued that having the "right action" was also equally important.

Right action was considered a part of the average person's willpower, in a world of indifference.

It was Zeno who argued that though things of this world may appear to be "morally indifferent" even in a world of indifference, there could be found a certain degree of goodness. Zeno would argue that "health, wealth, and beauty" would all be deemed to be good things and humanity ceaselessly strives for them.

But if someone happened to have none of these and was instead sick, poor, and homely—it did not necessarily mean they were a bad person as long as their intention was good. Zeno had essentially laid out the groundwork for a system of ethics that taught that the poorest man of the kingdom was just as good as the king if he had a good heart. Zeno maintained that morally indifferent forces outside of a human being's control, such as disease, his appearance, and perhaps even his economic status did not determine a man's goodness. And despite the hardship he faced, it was merely his "good intention" that would suffice.

This ethical determination launched by Zeno might seem rather common to us today. We all have probably heard someone say things like, "Well he meant well..." or perhaps if someone gave us a crummy gift for Christmas, even, "Well... it's the thought that counts..." As readily as we accept such standards today, they were revolutionary back in the ancient Hellenistic world.

The idea that someone poor and destitute, and sleeping on the street, could have just as good of intentions as an emperor seated on a throne, was a clarion call for moral equality that would have reverberations throughout all of civilization over the next couple thousand years. Early Christians would thoroughly identify with Zeno's understanding of moral equivalency, when Christianity later became the official religion of the Roman Empire.

Christians taught the same sort of equality, with the Apostle Paul famously declaring, in Galatians 3:28, "There is neither Jew nor Greek, there is neither slave nor free, there is no male and female, for you are all one in Christ Jesus." The obvious difference between Paul's take on this moral equality is he presents us all as moral equals under Jesus Christ. But even before Christianity, the stoics were hammering out what it meant to have true equality.

Christians today would also be familiar with the Stoic ethic of believing that "goodness" was the only long-lasting happiness. Other things of this world can be easily taken away. Both wealth and health could fail us, but being good to one another is a virtue that has lasting value. The ethics of the stoics asserts that man has both a natural and a moral life. The natural life being the natural impulses such as eating, drinking, finding a mate, and the like.

Moral life however, involves using reason to override more base physical impulses.

Chrysippus argued however that these two intersected because man was quite naturally endowed with reason in the first place, and since it is through reason that a "moral life" is established, moral life in itself is actually quite natural to begin with. If you find some of these thought exercises a little hard to follow at times, don't feel bad.

The ancient Greek philosophers—and most especially the Stoics, were quite famous for their circular logic and often going around in circles, arguing from one direction all the way to the other. This of course is all a legacy of the Socratic method established by Socrates himself which teaches us to logically debate not only with others, but even with ourselves, until we come to the best conclusion possible.

Speaking of circles, it was Hierocles, an orthodox Stoic who lived in the 2nd Century AD, who famously drew up a diagram of concentric circles in order to demonstrate the nature of how most view themselves and the world around them. They say a picture is worth a thousand words, and in the case of Hierocles, his little exercise most certainly proved this to be the case.

In the center of the circles was one solitary figure, representing one human being and their own individual thoughts and concerns with life. Inside this man's own personal bubble were his own personal impulses and needs.

In the most immediate circle next to him was a circle in which his wife, children, parents, and brothers all resided, as an indication of how close these relations were to his heart.

A little further out was another circle which held further removed relations such as his aunts, uncles, and cousins. Even further out from this circle was the man's connection to his neighbors and general community. Even further afield to this, was the connection to his city, and then to neighboring cities. The circles kept distancing themselves further and further from the individual, until the furthest circle symbolized the figure's relationship with his fellow man in its entirety.

Using this diagram to demonstrate the degrees of separation that build between people, it was argued that it would be ethical to "contract the circles" and lessen the distance between people, thereby having us relate to our distant relatives just as we would close ones, and treat neighbors just like we would our own kin. In other words, Hierocles, hammered out that it was ethical to treat everyone equally.

One of the major premises of Stoic ethics is indeed to treat others equitably. But above all obtaining virtue was the goal. But just what is it we are talking about when we speak of virtue? For such a seemingly simple thing, it can be explained in numerous ways. And the stoics were sure to expound upon just about every single possibility there was. But the main point, was the same one Socrates himself made before Stoicism as a school of thought had even been established.

For it was Socrates that declared that to be virtuous was to seek "knowledge and wisdom." The academy too, asserted that when "a man who fully knows what is right must also do it." Knowledge brought accountability. Unlike a small child who may not firmly understand right and wrong—a grown man who intrinsically knows that it is wrong to lie, murder, and steal, should be held accountable, not to do those very things.

It was the Cynics on the other hand who stressed that this awareness could not be actuated without self-discipline. They believed that it took practice to be able to resist bad behavior, and the more a person "resisted temptation" in one instance, the easier they would be able to in the next.

In other words, they viewed that virtue was like a muscle that could be flexed and strengthened by repeated use over time. The Stoics readily accepted this view, finding that virtue was indeed acquired through trial and error and it took practice to perfect over the course of one's life. Interestingly enough, the old expression "practice makes perfect" can actually be traced right back to Stoicism in this regard.

As such, the Ethics of Stoicism Can be summed up in 4 Main Virtues: wisdom, courage, justice, temperance.

Wisdom

The Stoics defined wisdom as being able to differentiate right from wrong. Someone with the Stoic brand of wisdom for example, would know that it was wrong to take advantage of others. They know intuitively that such behavior is *unethical*. They also know how to refrain from doing something on a mere impulse, because they have enough wisdom not to not be swayed by momentary passions or desires.

Stoicism stresses the pursuit of virtue to attain happiness, and the only way to discern virtue from vice is through having the wisdom to know the difference in the first place. Wisdom stands out from the other virtues as being purely theoretical in scope. As strange as it might sound, wisdom remains in theory because we cannot prove "that we know what we do not know."

We can say we know right from wrong, but in some sense, the idea is a relative one and depends upon perspective. What may be unethical for one person could be a good thing for another. So perhaps a better explanation of wisdom is to have knowledgeable discernment of what is really at stake in life and how to direct our own behavior accordingly.

Courage

Many of us tend to view those who demonstrate a courageous response as being the polar opposite of those who exhibit fear. But the Stoics didn't exactly see it that way. For them courage didn't mean that you would never be scared, for the Stoic philosopher displaying courage was a concerted act made *even if you are scared.* In other words, if a madman pulls a gun on your family, and you rush forward to tackle him—this act was courageous not because you were fearless, but simply because it forced you to act regardless of any fear you may have had. Or as it has otherwise been defined, courage is "doing the right thing even if we are afraid" to do it.

Much has been said of the "fight or flight" response, that people go through when faced with danger, but there is actually a third option in the works, making it "fight, flight, or freeze." Because fear can paralyze you. There are those who have literally lost their lives because they gave in to fear.

Just think of a pilot facing turbulence in the air, who panics so much he can't think of what he's doing. Alarms are going off in the cabin, and air traffic control is trying to give him very specific instructions on how to get through the storm. The pilot attempts to follow these directives but panics, freezes up, and the plane crashes into the ocean as a result.

Stoics did not teach people they needed to never be afraid, on the contrary they taught we should not give in to fear.

The fear is there, but by displaying the virtue of courage we can rationally work through it. Panaetius took this argument even further arguing that courage is not just "freedom from fear" but freedom from our lusts and desires.

Because for Panaetius one is not just showing courage when they climb the mountain and slay the dragon, one is equally courageous when they can stand firm in the face of worldly enticement. Imagine the business man who was just offered millions of dollars in kickbacks if he would simply compromise some of the standards his company abides by.

That money could have had him set for life, but he stood by his by his principles and rejected the offer. This is exactly the kind of moral courage that Panaetius is speaking of. By showing courage, one is able to resist the temptation exerted upon them by external factors and continue to stand firm in their own convictions and resolve.

Justice

In today's world when one think of justice, they most likely think of the packed courtrooms of the justice system that presides over the societies in which we live.

The Stoics saw it a little differently however, they viewed justice not so much as a legalistic matter in the courtroom but as an everyday experience.

They felt it was up to each and every individual to make sure justice was done to those around them.

This justice wasn't just over criminal matters either, but in regard to just about every interaction we had on a daily basis. Seeking the virtue of justice meant that you always tried to be fair and balanced with everyone you encountered. It also meant "giving back to the community" from which one lived rather than simply using up all the resources for yourself.

It is the virtue of justice that should serve as the "moral compass" that will guide you throughout everything you do. It is said that a sense of justice naturally "arises from the social instincts." It is argued these instincts can be placed on a sliding scale depending on the size of the community that it is in reference to; ranging from a close-knit family, to a city, to a nation, to the entire planet. Whatever the case may be, justice is viewed as the social instinct that "binds good men together."

It has been said the Stoic teaching of the virtue of justice has been especially useful for those who are in positions of leadership, teaching them to be more equitable to those who are under their employ. This was most certainly true for the great philosopher king, the Roman Emperor, Marcus Aurelius, who was careful to consider the virtue of justice, in just about everything he did.

Temperance

Have you ever heard the expression, "Moderation in all things?" In a nutshell, this is basically what the virtue of temperance is all about. Temperance is the ability of someone to resist their short-term urges, in favor of achieving more long-term goals. The virtue of temperance teaches self-control. Just because you want something, doesn't mean you have to have it. The Stoic by nature is able use their impulses to deny their impulses whenever it is necessary.

And it also helps one realize what they have in life. As the later stoic philosopher Seneca would describe it, "Until we have begun to go without then we fail to realize how unnecessary many things are. We've been using them not because we needed them but because we had them."

Just as Seneca told us, a little bit of temperance goes quite a long way when it comes to making sure we are not so consumed by pleasure, that we lose sight of what's really important in life.

Chapter 5: The 10 Principles of Stoicism You Need to Know

Stoicism can be a lot to take in at first glance, but there are several guiding principles that can help guide you through some of the confusion that you may initially experience. For those unaccustomed to some of the terminology and rhetoric, Stoicism can seem quite alien. But the interesting thing is; once you get to the core of what Stoicism actually stood for, most in the Western world will find that the core principles of Stoicism are basically wrapped up in a universal code of conduct that has been practiced all over the world.

Just think of "practice makes perfect"—how many times have you heard of that? Well, it was a Stoic concept long before anyone else used it. And what about, "Everything in moderation"—where did that come from? Well, it's nothing short of one of the main virtues of stoic philosophy. Having that said, we are going to delve even deeper into such tried and true principles, so that we can make what might have been initially unfamiliar, much more familiar to you. So without further ado, here are the top 10 principles of Stoicism that you need to know.

Use Your Own Judgement

The number one principle for Stoics, is the principle of judgement. And no—it's not a clarion call to make it our personal mission to go around judging people. We certainly have enough of that in the world as it is! On the contrary, for Stoics having the right kind of judgement meant being able to appropriately respond in any given situation and even suspend our judgment if need be.

According to this principle, one of the ultimate goals of Stoicism is to learn to react to our own rational judgement rather than simply having a kneejerk response to whatever comes our way. The Roman Emperor, turned Stoic philosopher Marcus Aurelius, perhaps said it best when he stated, "If any external thing causes you distress, it is not the thing itself that troubles you, but your own judgment about it. And this you have the power to eliminate now."

Perhaps American President Franklin Delano Roosevelt when addressing the nation during the Great Depression, was channeling Marcus Aurelius a bit when he declared, "There is nothing to fear but fear itself!" Because Marcus was saying much the same thing.

The basic takeaway from all this is that no matter what happens, we should not get so overwhelmed that we become a mindless reactionary to external events outside of our immediate control. If you accidentally rear-end a car in traffic for example, you shouldn't get out and start sobbing over what happened, instead you need to take proactive measures to make the situation better.

When you were a kid there's probably been occasions in which someone told you, "don't cry over spilled milk." Well, that's actually a very Stoic thing to say. In other words, what's done is done, you can't change external events that occur, but you can use your own mind, your own judgment, to rationally figure out the best way to move forward. Accord to Stoic philosophy, rather than just immediately reacting on impulse, we should go through three stages in response to any crisis.

In real time, it should go something like this; *an incident occurs, we judge or size up the situation, and then we react.* Do you see the difference? Instead of immediately reacting without thinking about the consequences, the Stoic takes time to consider the situation before responding. Having that said, of course, not all situations would give you much time for reflection.

If someone was coming at you with a baseball bat, for example, you just might have to default to regular old fight or flight.

Because if you stand there in deep thought and contemplation for too long while a bat-wielding maniac takes pot-shots at you, the consequences might not be too good. But having that said, in most other situations in life, you should be able to have enough time to judge the circumstances of an incident before you immediately react to it.

And where this principle of Stoicism really shines is in everyday, common interaction. Because there are plenty of times in which we interact with people, that we have bad reactions which may not be as visceral as the aforementioned bat-wielding assailant, but due to our own response can become just as devastating. Let's say for example you are in the breakroom at your workplace and you feel that one of your coworkers has slighted you.

It's certainly not a life or death situation, but its unpleasant enough to provoke a severe reaction all the same. And many in the heat of the moment, will react without thinking, and say something that they may seriously regret later on. Such a situation presents the perfect time to employ the Stoic principle of judgment. Those with no judgement—let alone impulse control—might end up going off on their coworker in a profanity laced tirade.

What would be the result of all this? Most likely that employee would soon be looking for another line of work.

And what did they gain by their actions?

While standing in the unemployment line, they would most likely tell you—*nothing at all.* Having that said, if someone offends, instead of immediately reacting, you need to learn to step back from the situation, consider all of the factors involved, and then proceed with the most rational response in light of the circumstances.

In order to have a Stoic frame of mind, you need to avoid being prompted and prodded by external stimulus. Instead of having kneejerk reactions to outside forces, you should be able to look within yourself for how you respond, and not be so easily malleable to outside factors. With good judgement we learn to make better use of our own mind rather than being influenced by the actions and opinions of others.

Just to drive this point home, let's return to the scenario of someone dealing with a coworker's slight in the workplace. If someone immediately reacts in anger or pain, it means the rudeness of their associate is of great importance to them. It's amazing sometimes how important we place the opinions of other people—even people we don't particularly care for—above our own.

By angrily responding to a colleague's rude remarks, you are actually giving them weight.

By placing importance on your coworker's critiques, you are making the judgement, whether intentionally or unintentionally, that the opinion of this person matters. Instead, you can step back, ponder the situation and come to the conclusion this troublesome individual's words mean nothing and their opinion is completely irrelevant.

It takes a strong mind with good judgement to be able to avoid being ensnared by outside agitators who seek to disturb you. The key thing to take away from this, is to realize we are in control of our actions and we can control how we react to whatever comes our way. In considering this, I can remember the words of my own father, who used to advise me along much the same lines, telling me, "You can't control others. The only one you can control is yourself."

I guess my old man was a Stoic and he didn't even know it, because that statement perfectly sums up what it means to abide by the Stoic principle of judgment. Having that said, it's amazing how *out of control* people are anymore. All you have to do is turn on the news—or better yet drive down the street! And you will see plenty of people having a very hard time controlling their own actions.

There are terrible cases of road rage each and every day where folks lose their mind over the smallest (or in some instances even imaginary) infractions of other motorists. In order to avoid this fate, we all need to step back and use our better judgment as much as we possibly can.

Even though we may all want to change the world—it's much easier to change ourselves first.

Because as this Stoic principle confirms, our experiences in life very much revolve around our own innate judgement. In Stoicism, much of how we respond to any given situation is not so much generated by those around us as it is determined by what's inside of us. In other words, it's our own judgements (or lack thereof) that determines the outcomes of our interactions.

For those who are used to constantly reacting without thinking, learning to step back and make rational judgement might be challenging at first. It could seem like our reactions our second nature, and that we are unable to modify them. According to the Stoic Seneca, the reason such things are so difficult is quite frankly, because one who does not harness the will of their judgement has grown "soft."

Or as Seneca put it, "When pleasures have corrupted both mind and body, nothing seems to be tolerable—not because the suffering is hard, but because the sufferer is soft. For why are we thrown into a rage by somebody's cough or sneeze, by negligence in chasing a fly away, by a dog that gets in the way, or by the dropping of a key that has slipped from the hand of a careless servant?"

Going back to our road rage example used earlier, Seneca would probably judge that modern folks have become so soft and entitled that they fly into a rage over the pettiest of things.

It's because we've had it so good in the modern world, that we are often ready to fly off the handle over absolutely nothing at all.

In a world in which the nerves of many are in a constant state of heightened alert, it can be hard not to react outright. But the more you engage in these sorts of mental exercises, the more adept you will become at using your own judgement to rationally respond to any challenge you may face.

In order to put Stoic principles to practice you need to be able to suspend your judgement long enough to assess things as they come. When we do so, we often find that something we previously viewed as intolerable is not nearly as bad as it first seemed.

Perhaps the Stoic, Roman Emperor, Marcus Aurelius said it best when he declared, "Today I escaped from anxiety. Or no, I discarded it, because it was within me, in my own perceptions; not outside. Take away your opinion, and there is taken away the complaint. Take away the complaint, and the hurt is gone."

Don't Be Affected by Externals

As you may have already noticed, much of what the Stoics taught revolved around fine tuning our reactions to the external environment. As mentioned earlier, Stoicism teaches us to be careful how we judge the situations we find ourselves in, so we don't get tripped up by them, and start acting badly.

And in Stoic speak, an "external" is anything that is beyond our own purview that we normally have no direct control over. The goal of stoicism is to face these external factors head-on "without attachment." And this is the classic feature that sets Stoics apart—their utter refusal to let things that they cannot control, ruin their day. In other words, Stoics do not let external factors determine the mood they are in.

And you most especially do not let the opinions of others affect the opinion you hold of yourself. Of course, there is some nuance to this, and there certainly is some exception to the rule. The opinion of one's spouse for example, would naturally have a little more weight than the random stranger on the street. But even so, one's happiness cannot completely hinge even on one's spouse.

The Stoic must be strongly grounded in their own self-worth and not be affected by any externalities. Stoicism also stresses that it is important not to be deceived by an externality that seems frightening or enticing enough to compel us act. Stoicism teaches us to look at externals rationally, and resist the urge to think that we have influence over things we really do not.

Because while we can indeed control our own judgment/opinions of a situation, we have no control over external events and we furthermore need to make sure we are not mistakenly convinced we do.

The Stoic needs to be relatively unmoved by outside pressure that tries to convince one to intervene.

Instead of being artificially affected and swayed one way or the other, the goal of the Stoic is to see things as they really are.

Or as Stoic philosopher Seneca described it, "So remember this above all, to strip away the disorder of things and to see what is in each of them; you will learn that nothing in them is frightening but the fear itself. What you see happening to boys, happens to us too. Their friends—the ones they are accustomed to and play with—if they see them wearing masks, they are terrified. The mask needs to be removed not just from people but from things, and the true appearance of each restored."

Seneca described irrational people to be like children who are startled when their playmates suddenly wear masks. According to Seneca, in a similar way, many of the outside externalities we face in this world, are not what they seem. And if we were to simply unmask them for what they are, our fears, anxieties, and perhaps even fascination, would quickly subside.

For a Stoic, it is absolutely imperative not to get overwhelmed by externalities, and instead keep things in perspective. Stoics therefore do not hedge their bets solely on snap judgement, but instead rely on their critical thinking ability to see matters clearly. In order to do so, Stoics teach to not project their own impressions on an external event. To illustrate this in action, take the following hypothetical as an example.

Let's say you are walking around at your local shopping mall and see a friend dining at a nearby food court. You look over at the person, expecting they might engage you. The person then looks up and briefly seems to make eye contact with you, but then quickly looks away. The sensitive person would most likely be offended. Their mind would start reeling with indignation as they proceed to project their most negative possible interpretation of the incident.

You think to yourself, "Did he just snub me? I know he saw me! What did I ever do to deserve being disrespected like that?" But these are all personal projections on an externality. In reality all you really know is that the person seemed to look at you and then for whatever reason, they looked away. Nothing more. Nothing less. But by projecting all of your anxieties and fears onto the event, suddenly the situation has become a major insult and affront, leaving you feeling as if you had just been treated terribly by someone who you thought was your friend.

These are all false creations of the observer however, and were artificially added to the externality. Now let's continue on with this scenario of the person who thought they were so rudely snubbed. Let's say the following week you bump into that person from the mall once again. Yet this time the reaction is much different. The friend walks right up, makes eye contact and has a big grin fills their face, they exclaim, "Hey man! Good to see you!"

Immediately you are in a quandary. Why are they so friendly all of the sudden? After they snubbed you like that at the mall? Shortly into the conversation however you find the answer, your best was not ignoring you after all, they had just undergone eye surgery, and had been having trouble making out faces from a distance. My, how the mask you put on that poorly judged externality, came falling right off! Now don't you feel silly?

And all of it was completely unnecessary in the first place. This faulty and detrimental understanding of external events, is precisely what the Stoic is trying to avoid. People often completely misinterpret events by adding their often mistaken first impressions onto them. Stoicism seeks to free us from this false narrative of our own creation. Stoics teach us to cast out our imaginations.

Curiously, this is yet another parallel with Christianity, and in particular, the Apostle Paul in the New Testament of the Christian Bible. Because when one reads 2nd Corinthians 10:5, which expresses the need for, "Casting down imaginations, and every high thing that exalteth itself against the knowledge of God, and bringing into captivity every thought to the obedience of Christ."

We can see that the similarity to Stoicism is quite uncanny. Yes, the Apostle Paul was indeed, basically saying the same exact thing as the Stoics!

He was advising not to project our ill-conceived "imaginations" onto external events!

And furthermore, to use knowledge and self-discipline to control our impulses!

The only difference is that Paul inserted God into the mix, whereas the stoics would simply have advised to cast down imagination that exalt (give false impressions) over knowledge (true discernment), and left it at that.

Paul may have added a religious tone to the message, but it's basically the same exact concept. For it is the Stoic belief that we should not give in to false impressions, imaginations, high-minded pretensions (every high thing that exalteth itself?) when attempting to assess external events.

The Stoic realizes that humanity has a propensity to seek and create all kinds of patterns in life. It's for this reason we look up and see faces in clouds, or even the fact that we draw lines between stars to create constellations. The point is—we naturally tend to connect the dots when there is nothing there. The funny thing is, all the while that we are doing this, we trick ourselves into thinking we are being rational.

Just like the example of the guy who thinks his friend snubbed him at the mall, we are taking bits and pieces of external data, putting them together, and trying to make sense of them. But as the aforementioned example demonstrates, the conclusions that we draw are often incredibly off base.

By nature, we are creatures who attempt to reason and make sense of our environment, but the Stoics knew full well that there were times that we might let our reasoning and speculation run amuck. The man who thought he was snubbed by his friend, *reasoned* that his friend looked right at him and then proceeded to look away. In his mind at the time, this was reason enough for him to conclude he had just been horribly insulted.

This is what he reasoned, but his reasoning or rationalizing of the external data he perceived was highly inaccurate. He of course had no way of knowing that his friend had just had eye surgery and the fact he couldn't see clear enough to recognize him, was the real reason that he looked away. The offended party didn't have this bit of crucial information so they let their mind go wild to connect dots that weren't there.

This is why Stoicism stresses to just see things exactly as they transpire and add nothing more, and nothing less. The Stoic would observe the same situation and simply report back that someone appeared to look at them and then looked away. There would be no dramatic conclusion that the action was a personal affront to the Stoic, merely that this was what had occurred.

Stoics choose not to overly exert themselves asking why things happen, they merely state the facts readily at hand and move on. The sooner you learn not to be affected by externals, the sooner you will be free from fruitless speculation. The embracing of this practice can be truly liberating for those who suffer from anxiety, since much of what we are anxious about are our own interpretations of the external environment. Take this principle to heart and you will not be troubled by such things anymore.

Keeping the Right Perspective

In Stoicism, there are two main methods of discernment that are typically employed. First, is the analytical method which entails suppressing our own snap judgments, and false impressions, so we can unmask externalities, and see them for what they are. The other method however, is an intuitive one that seeks to filter all experience through our own intuition in order to alter our perspective.

If you look at an issue from one angle, and then are simply able to shift your perspective, we are then able to remove ourselves from the equation so we can evaluate the situation in a state of detachment. The Stoics show us the mistake we make when we view our place in the universe, and our sense that we are somehow significant in the grand scheme of things.

Stoics contend that our inflated sense of ego is derived from our faulty perspective. By default, we tend to associate everything with how it relates to us and our situation. Things that occur during our finite life here on this planet seem like a big deal, but as the Stoics describe it, this is just a major misnomer on our part. The Stoic seeks to instill in us by our own intuition, how miniscule our petty concerns are when compared to the grand tapestry of creation.

These efforts are meant to make the budding Stoic a little humbler, and a virtuous life more appealing. Some might at first feel that looking upon human life as miniscule and often times, rather meaningless, would be a reason for depression. But on the contrary, Stoics, felt it was freeing and reassuring instead.

And the humbleness that such shifts in perspective bring about are rewarding for their ability to cure us of any lingering avarice, envy, strife, or misplaced priorities. By shifting the focus away from ourselves, it helps us to better look toward the greater good of humanity/existence.

Stoicism existed as a powerful movement from approximately 200 BC to 200 AD, and it's interesting to note that out of all the philosophies prevalent some 2,000 odd years ago, Stoicism was unique in its sense that humanity was insignificant.

At a time when most other belief systems had man as the center of the universe, with the sun, moon, planets, and stars literally revolving around the Earth—the Stoics held that man's place in the cosmos was as more of a sideshow, rather than being anywhere near center stage.

The Roman Emperor and esteemed Stoic philosopher, Marcus Aurelius perhaps summed it up best when he wrote, "Asia and Europe are corners of the universe; the whole of the sea is a drop in the universe; Athos, a tiny clod of dirt in the universe; all the present time is one point in eternity. Everything is small, easily changing; disappearing."

Marcus Aurelius was able to describe all the oceans of the planet as just a drop in the universe. This he managed to do thousands of years before space exploration enabled the likes of the famed astronomer Carl Sagan to come to much the same conclusion when he presented our whole entire planet as nothing more than a "pale blue dot suspended in a sunbeam."

It was on Valentine's Day, February 14th, 1990, when NASA's Voyager spacecraft soaring toward the edge of the solar system, famously looked back, and took a snapshot of the Earth from nearly 4 billion miles away. The image of the planet which took up less than a pixel in the photo, revealed, as Carl Sagan put it, that, "the Earth is a very small stage in a vast cosmic arena."

As Sagan rightly described, seeing the Earth, the entire sum total of human history and aspiration presented as nothing more than a miniscule dot in the vacuum of space does much to change your perspective of things. But the Stoics didn't need NASA to tell them this. They already intuitively knew it! And the fact that an ancient Stoic could have such a powerful sense of perspective is rather remarkable.

Perhaps Mr. Sagan was inspired by Marcus in the first place, because as one continues to read through Marcus Aurelius' meditations, you can find yet another chief example of this Stoic perspective that strikes an even more similar sounding refrain.

Because it was Marcus Aurelius who had declared, "The Earth with its cities and peoples, its rivers and encircling sea, if measured by the universe, we may regard as a mere dot. Our life occupies a portion smaller than a dot, if it is compared with all of time, because the measure of eternity is greater than that of the world; the world recreates itself over and over within the bounds of time." Less than a pixel, smaller than a dot, however you look at it—one's perspective is forever changed in the knowledge of how finite our world really is.

Reigning in Desire/Passion

One of the main, prevailing themes of Stoicism is that unhappiness is the result of how we perceive/judge our hopes and concerns for tomorrow, in relation to the joy and sorrow of today. In order to better navigate through this potential minefield, the Stoic must learn how to use logical reasoning.

And it stands to reason, that most of us tend to want things that we don't have. Whether it's that job promotion that's out of reach, that luxurious mansion up on the hill, or whatever the case may be—us human beings tend to yearn for the things that we lack rather than counting on all the blessing we currently have at our disposal. The Stoic's argue however, that the idea that we even want any of these things is a false narrative we have created.

And in reality, it's not that we want these bigger and better things, it's that *we think we want them*. Because most of the time when people acquire something they yearn for, they're not satisfied, and it's not long before they start looking for something else. So, keeping this in mind, it's the Stoics who contend that what really drives most of us is the pursuit of goals and objects we think will make us happy, rather than the end result itself.

In other words, we are enamored with the thrill of the chase, but by the time we corner our prize, like a cat bored with a caught mouse, we're ready to cast it to the side. This is why highly successful people, millionaires and billionaires and the like, are often some of the most miserable individuals you could ever meet. They've been to the top of the mountain and have become bored with the view. That object we so yearned for, is now repugnant to us at worst, and absolutely meaningless at best.

Stoics called this lack of satisfaction, the "insatiability of desires." According to Stoicism, our desires are insatiable. We are never satisfied. The more things we acquire in life, the more we feel like we lack. We keep wanting bigger and better things. What we have is never enough. Like an addict in need of a fix, sometimes success itself can be a drug with the individual driven to reach a high mark that seems to get higher each and every achievement they make.

This is why for a Stoic the reining in of our desires/passion is so important. In later stoicism much emphasis is placed on this, and inflamed passion is even likened to a being a "disease" that needs to be eradicated. Stoic leader, Chrysippus was a definite proponent of this, charging that continually giving way to one's passion would lead to a "diseased state of mind" in which a perpetual false narrative is created.

It was perhaps the Stoic philosopher Epictetus who said it best when he declared, "Don't you know how thirst works in someone with a fever? It is nothing like the thirst of a man in good health. He drinks and is no longer thirsty. The sick man is happy only for a moment, then is nauseous; he converts the drink into bile, he vomits, his stomach hurts, and then he is thirstier still. It is just like this to crave riches and have riches, to crave power and have power, to crave a beautiful woman and sleep with her."

In order to escape the endless cycle of pursuit that Epictetus describes, one must gain control of their impulses and blunt their desires, lest they be overtaken by them completely.

Learning to Live in the Present

Stoicism teaches a form of mindfulness, that seeks to have its adherents live in the present rather than dwelling on the past or fearing the future. Stoics would remind their pupils that what's done is done—you can't go back in time to correct mistakes of the past. Likewise, you can't jump ahead and know the future. Therefore, it was consistently taught that one should do their best to live in the present. For a Stoic who practiced living in the present, each new day was basically a "reset" on their whole existence.

There was no sadness over what happened yesterday or dread over what may happen tomorrow, stoics simply lived in the now and took things as they came.

You might recall from earlier in this book when we mentioned the example of Cato the Younger. Cato was attacked by a man in a Roman bathhouse. The next day however, he completely put it out of his mind. So much so, that when his assailant even apologized for the previous day's actions, Cato claimed he didn't even remember it. Choosing to forget the past, Cato was living for the present.

The Stoic must dispel any lingering doubts about the past or fear of the future. As Seneca put it, "Two things we must therefore root out: fear of distress in the future and the memory of distress in the past. The one concerns me no longer. The other concerns me not yet."

In other words, the past is over, so why worry about it? And at the same time the future hasn't happened yet, so there is no need fretting over future events.

Instead of getting ahead in life, many of us feel as if we are stuck on a treadmill, always struggling to keep up. We look back at the past and feel that we haven't accomplished enough, and yet we dread the future, fearing that our efforts will fall short. The Stoic however, breaks this cycle by living in the moment, and refusing to entertain doubts of the past, or fears of the future either one. The Stoic simply keeps putting one foot in front of the other, and takes life as it comes.

Not Being Overcome by Emotion

Even though Stoics carry the well-known stereotype of "being stoic"—Stoicism is not as devoid of emotion as people think. In fact, stoicism encourages emotion. It just needs to be used in a productive fashion. Because as Stoic philosopher Seneca explained it, "I should not be unfeeling like a statue; I should care for my relationships both natural and acquired—as a pious man, a son, a brother, a father, [and] a citizen."

So just what kind of emotive expression do the Stoic philosophers recommend? Emotions should only be expressed so much as they don't disrupt our ability to think rationally. As a rule, the Stoics determine whether or not their emotion exceeds its bounds, by virtue of how much they disturb our internal equilibrium. If, for example, someone is extremely upset about an issue, they will most likely have trouble making logical decisions.

And likewise, if someone is so enamored with an externality that it affects their decision-making process, their judgement on that matter should not be trusted.

Any overwhelming emotion that could be perceived as a threat to sound judgment should be avoided. Having that said, Stoics acknowledged there were some cases—despite how one might try—in which not being overcome by emotions might indeed be hard thing to do.

Or as Seneca famously put it, when discussing this matter with a colleague of his, "There are certain things, Lucilius, that no courage can avoid; nature reminds courage of its own mortality. And so, the courageous man will frown at sad things; he will be startled by a sudden occurrence; he will feel dizzy if, standing at the brink, he looks down from the precipice. This is not fear but a natural feeling not to be overcome by reason."

We are only human after all, and if placed in a shocking enough circumstance even the best of Stoics could be caught off guard. Seneca expounded upon this further by describing such instances as merely a "momentary lapse of reason." Seneca stated, "An emotion, then does not consist in being moved by the appearances of things but in surrendering to them and following up this casual impulse. For if anyone supposes that turning pale, bursting into tears, sexual arousal, deep sighs, flashing eyes, and anything of that sort are a sign of emotion and mental state, he is mistaken and does not understand that these things are merely bodily impulses. A man thinks himself injured, wants to be revenged, and then being dissuaded for some reason—he quickly calms down again. I don't call this anger, but a mental impulse yielding to reason."

For the Stoic, having firm control of our emotional drives is of the utmost importance. Many are unduly blinded by their emotions and provoked to respond in ways that might not be in their best interest. We need to be in the driver's seat at all times in order to avoid impulsive behavior.

Having that said however, even the Stoics recognized that there are occasions in which controlling one's emotions would be harder than others. If for example, you just received word one of your loved ones had passed away, even a Stoic wouldn't begrudge you for bursting into tears. Seneca for one, accepted such things as a natural consequence of human nature.

The difference between how a Stoic and a non-Stoic handles such things however is a Stoic makes sure not to wallow in grief, as soon as the natural wave of emotion passes over, the Stoic returns to a state of reason, refraining from being overcome any further by emotional excess.

Overcoming Fear of Death

In Stoic philosophy, death is the ultimate external event. Short of suicide, we have no way to naturally control when we die. As such, death is usually viewed with fear. Since Stoic philosophy seeks to alleviate such feelings with reason, it is no wonder they would spend considerable time and energy seeking to overcome the fear of death.

In contemplation of death Stoics reason that the most frightening part of death for most, is simply the mystery involved in it.

But having that said, the actual end result, according to the Stoics, "leaves us no worse off than we were before we were born." Stoics furthermore contend that death is a "continuous" and "natural" process that takes place over the course of one's life.

Death therefore, should be feared no more than birth, or any other natural part of existence in this world. Stoics believed that fear of death was due to lack of reason, and overcoming this fear with rational analysis was a liberating experience. But much more than just seeking to free the adherent from their fear of death, Stoics taught their pupils that death was a great agent for gaining insight and even encouragement. As the Stoics saw it, "mortality is the defining feature of our existence."

We are indeed here for a short time. Just the very thought of how finite our life is, brings new perspective and meaning to what we should be doing during our brief period of existence.

It is for this reason that Stoics were known to "meditate on death" in order to produce certain virtues such as humbleness, courage, and temperance. The Stoics sought to unmask death, and see it for what it truly was—simply a natural result of life.

According to Stoicism, despite the fear that the notion of death generates, death was not necessarily a bad thing in itself.

Or as Seneca described it, "Death belongs among those things that are not evils in truth, but still have an appearance of evil; for a love of self is implanted in us, and a desire of existence and survival, and a dread of disintegration.

Death seems to rob us of many good things and to remove us from all we have come to know. And there is another element that estranges us from death we are already familiar with the present, but are ignorant of the future into which we will go, and we shrink from the unknown. Even if death is something indifferent, then it is nevertheless a thing that cannot be easily ignored."

As Seneca acknowledged, death is not easy to dismiss, but as the Stoics taught, with concerted concentration, we can work to overcome much of our fear of death and dying. And perhaps it was Seneca who said it best when he declared, "What is death? A mask to frighten children. Turn it and examine it. See, it does not bite. The poor body must be separated from the spirit as it was before, either now or later. Why then are you troubled if it be now?"

As has been mentioned a few times in this book, there are striking similarities between Stoic perspectives and early Christianity. Seneca's take on death provides us with another one, since the Apostle Paul clearly seconded his opinion when in the Book of 1st Corinthians, he too declared, "Death! Where is thy sting!" The concept of death takes up much thought in the world of the living, but the sooner we unmask it, much of that initial sting—the fear of death—does indeed go out of it.

The Stoics of antiquity themselves, lived in a very uncertain world.

The average lifespan was much shorter than what we enjoy today and the chance of dying from injury or disease was much greater. As such, the Stoics felt it rather expedient to teach their followers to lose their fear of death early on. By ridding themselves of this ever-present facet of their external environment they could then free themselves to pursue life in its fullest.

Dealing with Adversity

Just like everyone else, Stoics do not look forward to adversity. Unnecessary hardship is certainly not something that they actively seek out. Nevertheless, when adversity does come their way, they strive to prevent themselves from becoming overly affected by it. On the contrary, despite any difficulty, for a Stoic, adversity is seen as a potential opportunity in which they can use adversity to improve their disposition.

Stoics view hard times as a kind of proving ground, like the fires in a forge which help to shape and mold them into a stronger, better person. In this Stoics are seeking to find inherent benefit, even in what might initially appear to be undesirable situations. The stoics view adversity in the same way that they view death. They view it as an often-misunderstood external factor, that if harnessed appropriately, could be used for good.

Stoics contend that something is a hardship for us, simply because we perceive it that way. But if we would just suspend our judgement and step back for a moment, we just might see that what we are facing was not as bad as it may have appeared at first glance. And what's more, there may even be some intrinsic good in what previously appeared to be entirely bad.

Once again, it all boils down to the basic Stoic teaching that even though we have no control over many external events, we can indeed control how we respond to them. As such, whenever hardship arises, the Stoic attempts to make it into a teaching moment, in order to better themselves. Also, since Stoicism advises that our first impressions are often mistaken, a slow approach to analyzing a hardship is used, in case it turns out to be a true blessing in disguise.

When faced with certain kinds of adversity, Stoics will also often try to put themselves into the shoes of others, and shift their perspective enough to see the situation differently. With these changes in perspective, the hardship often does not appear as bad at first glance.

Stoic Philosopher Seneca described as much, when he said, "Do you think that the wise man is burdened by evils? He makes use of them.

It was not only from ivory that Phidias knew how to make statues; he made them also from bronze.

If you had given him marble, or some still lesser material, he would have carved the best statue that could be made of it.

So the wise man will display virtue amid riches if possible, but if not, in poverty; at home if he can, but if not, in exile; as a general if he can, but if not, as a solder; in sound health if he can, but if not, then in weakness. Whatever fortune he is dealt, he will make of it something remarkable."

Yes, according to the Stoics, adversity is truly what you make of it. If you feel that the hardships are insurmountable, they will remain so. But if you look toward them as redefining moments, you can learn to adjust. And the sooner you do, the more successful you will be. As soon as any adversity emerges, instead of shrinking away from the challenge, you should face it head-on.

Don't be Blinded by Greed and Pleasure

Much of Stoic doctrine speaks at length over how we can learn to control both our perceptions and our impulses, desires, and passions. All human beings of course desire the good things in life, but the Stoics issue stern warnings for those who would be consumed by gluttony and greed.

According to Stoicism, anything that a man may have unchecked avarice for, he could later become ensnared by.

The Stoics caution their followers to not be so blinded by the greed of this world that they lose sight of what's important.

According to this principle of Stoicism, greed, and the love of riches has the propensity to create quite a bit of strife in our lives.

The Stoics contend that greed usually follows a typical pattern. Someone obtains things that they greatly value, but are not satisfied. Instead they immediately have fear and doubt should they lose their precious commodity. Not only that, they are also desirous of more of it, never satiated with what they actually have.

As well as being applicable to material riches, the same thing could be applied to any perceived pleasure in life. There are countless people out there who are addicted to physical and emotional pleasures and these addictions more or less follow the same patterns that the Stoics outlined. Just look at any given addiction; whether it be drugs, alcohol, food, gambling, or even relationships.

They all can succumb to this unhealthy cycle of desire, fear of loss, and yearning for more of the same. Just take the example of a domineering, abusive husband. At first glance one might think such a person hates their wife, due to the way they treat them. But in reality, that person greatly values their spouse like a prized commodity, and therefore seeks to obsessively control everything they do.

This person has an irrational fear of losing their spouse, so they seek to dominate them entirely.

At the same time the domineering husband might also have a wandering eye and cultivate other relationships elsewhere, because despite their tyrannical hold on their own spouse, deep down they are not satisfied and yearn for further fulfillment.

In order to remedy such a situation, the Stoic would once again stress moderation. Stoics recommend a slight detachment from the things we desire, in order to prevent greed. We need to resist chasing after rewards, and refrain from clinging from them once we have them. And we need to strengthen our resolve not to become completely devastated if we were to lose them, as this is an externality and all externals are ultimately uncertain in the end.

Seneca perhaps summed this sentiment up best when he remarked, "He who has need of riches feels fear on their account. But no man enjoys a blessing that brings anxiety. He is always trying to add a little more. While he puzzles over increasing his wealth, he forgets how to use it."

We need to learn to appreciate what's in our hand and not seek out more than we actually need. Marcus Aurelius was probably one of the best experts on this Stoic Mindset since he was the all-powerful ruler of the Roman Empire. One can only imagine the wealth and excess that most have been at his disposal. Yet, Marcus was one was always sure to keep any propensity for greed in check.

Even though he could have lived a lavish life he usually opted for austerity. Instead of wearing expensive clothes, he wore the most basic of tunics. Rather than be a glutton for fine wine and expensive food, he only consumed what was necessary. Marcus Aurelius knew full well how to avoid being blinded by greed and excess pleasure, and the modern Stoic would do well to follow his example.

Don't Worry About What Others Think

For Stoics, it is very important to learn how to avoid being affected by the outside world. And a major part of this is through not worrying too much over what others might think. Stoics realize that we all seek approval from others in various ways, but Stoicism calls for us to avoid such "vanity and pride." Stoics identify such things as yearning for recognition by externals; friends, family, and the like. We all want to be accepted, but Stoicism teaches us to have "contempt for conformity."

Never mind what everyone else thinks, the Stoic only does what they themselves believes to be right. Sadly, most people do not fall into this category. Most do indeed live by a certain amount of groupthink; the dangerous excesses of which have been seen all throughout history.

Just think of any atrocity committed in the past few centuries and you will find that every day, average people did awful things just to conform with what others in society were doing.

Everyone else was doing it, so they felt that either it must be right, or they had simply no choice but to conform, lest they stand out and become targets themselves. Go to any war crimes trial and you will no doubt hear more than one person make the claim that they were simply, "following orders."

Stoics completely reject the idea that human beings are social lemmings who have to follow what others are doing. Stoics acknowledge however, that breaking away from the pack can be difficult. And that the prevailing opinions of any given society often does pressure the individual to conform. But Stoicism calls for resistance all the same. In order to do this, Stoics call for their followers to not have an "appetite for praise" since it is in seeking the accolades of others that we become lackeys to social directives.

Instead of seeking approval from others, the Stoic has to stop and ask, "Why do I care if they like what I'm doing or not?" For a Stoic it is natural to develop skepticism of prevailing public opinion. Stoics are fully aware most people fail to use their own critical thinking and are easily swayed by public pressure. As such, public consensus does not hold much weight with them.

Instead Stoics argue that it is better to trust one's own judgment and not worry about what others may think as a consequence. The Stoic uses their own mind to decide what is right and their decisions are not based on the desires of others.

As none other than a Roman Emperor named Marcus Aurelius put it, "The part of the good man is not to peer into the character of others, but to run straight down the line without glancing one side or the other." The Stoic needs to be a straight shooter, know their own convictions and do what's right—no matter what anyone else might think about it.

Chapter 6: How to Practice Stoicism in Modern Life

Although Stoicism got its start well over 2000 years ago, its practices and principles can and do still apply to modern life. The Stoics were themselves students of life. They studied every idiosyncrasy of human behavior and thought, seeking to perfect how they approached their own existence. Having that said, they developed a wealth of knowledge that is still relevant to us to this very day. Here in this chapter we will explore further how one might better apply the practice of stoicism in modern life.

Make Use of Mentors

Stoicism was founded by inspirational figures and continued to be led by them for centuries. As such, in classical stoicism, the adherent to the practice had no shortage of mentors and role models in the movement. These veterans of Stoicism would answer any questions their pupils may have had and more importantly they led by example, visibly demonstrating to them what a virtuous life was all about.

Even though there aren't exactly learned Stoics on every corner in the modern age, there are still plenty of smart and successful people that could serve as a mentor.

You just might find that many of the most successful people in society practice aspects of Stoicism and don't even know it. So, in this sense, you should find those that seem to be living up to the Stoic ideals of virtue and use them as your personal mentors and role models.

In times of difficulty think of this person and how they might approach the same hardship. You can even do a little thought exercise in your mind by openly asking yourself—what would my mentor do? As the Stoic philosopher Seneca recommended, "Choose someone whose way of life as well as words have won your approval. Be always painting him out to yourself either as your guardian or as your model. There is a need, in my view, for someone as a standard against which our characters can measure themselves. Without a ruler to do it against you won't make crooked straight."

In other words, we need good examples to compare ourselves to and use as our "ruler" so that we can make sure that our own lives turn out alright. Make use of good mentors whenever you can in life. Mentors are those that have been through life's challenge and survived to tell about it. It would do you some good to follow their lead.

Negative Visualization

Perhaps you have been in a bad situation before and overheard someone say, "Well—it could be worse!" Whether that person realized it or not, by making such a rationalization they were engaging in the ancient Stoic practice of "negative visualization." Just as it sounds, when things go wrong, this practice has us consider how much worse things could have been.

Even if nothing bad has happened, negative visualization is also useful as a cognitive exercise for prepping yourself for unforeseen contingencies. Let's say you have to get up in front of all of the people you work with and give a speech. You're nervous about the event and wonder what might go wrong. Well according to Stoicism, instead of casting those thoughts aside, embrace them!

Take the time to do a negative visualization and consider in depth all the things that could go horribly wrong! Yep, that's right. Find a comfortable chair and some quiet time and let your mind wander directly to that upcoming event that you've been dreading. Now think about all the missteps you might potentially make. What if your nervous? What if you stumble with your words? What if the audience is rude and people start laughing at you or making snide remarks? What if your boss judges you harshly? And the list goes on and on.

Consider all of these negative outcomes as if they had just actually happened and then imagine how you might react to them. That way by the time the event arrives, even if any of your fears come true, your negative visualization will help you be well prepared for it.

Seneca was a proponent of this technique, as was demonstrated when he remarked, "What is quite unlooked for is more crushing in its effect, and unexpectedness adds to the weight of a disaster. The fact that it was unforeseen has never failed to intensify a person's grief. This is a reason for ensuring that nothing ever takes us by surprise. We should project our thoughts ahead of us at every turn and have in mind every possible eventuality instead of only the usual course of events." We all have anxieties from time to time in life. But much of it is due to worrying about things that are either out of our control, or having even happened yet. So, what's the worst that could happen? Engage in negative visualization to find out! You will quickly find that things aren't as bad as you first thought, and even if they are—you will be better equipped to handle any contingency that might arise.

Engage in Occasional Voluntary Discomfort

Sometimes we just don't know how good we have it in life. And a prime way to realize this, is to engage in occasional voluntary discomfort. What does that mean? It means every once in a while, depriving yourself of certain things whether that be food, companionship, or comfort—it could do you some good to engage in a bit of deprivation every so often.

That way if the situation were to arise in which you were forcibly deprived of something, the blow would not be as hard when it happened. Not only will engaging in occasional discomfort help toughen you up in case of future hardship, many find it also helps them become more thoughtful and creative as a result. Sometimes you just need to get just a little uncomfortable in order to have a better perspective of who you are and what you need to do.

This is precisely why so many religions have their members engage in fasting. Not only is this a sign of faith but it also serves to get the faithful more focused on what's important in life. By depriving themselves of food, their minds are sharpened and their senses are enhanced. Ancient Stoics used to do all manner of things in order to get in this same exact state.

Some would sleep out on the open ground outside, just to render enough hardship to give them a better perspective on life. Even Marcus Aurelius, Emperor of the Roman Empire is said to have on occasion, declined comfortable bedding in favor of sleeping on the bare floor. And while no one is suggesting you snuggle up with your floorboards when you go to sleep at night, it's good to be able to get out of your personal comfort space from time to time.

Acknowledge and Learn to Love Your Fate

In a world of chaos and disorder, the Stoics always put emphasis on self-control, since at the end of the day, it is only one's own actions that they are in control of. Having that said, as it pertained to an often-chaotic world outside, the Stoic instructed their pupils to not fret over the way things were but instead to learn to love the circumstances they were dealt, and accept them out of hand.

Since much of our ultimate fate is beyond our control, the Stoics teach that we might as well make the best of it. Have you ever heard the phrase, "Just go with the flow?" This is a very stoic saying, since it sums up this practice.

nThe more you struggle against the pull of external forces the more you are going to suffer. But as soon as you accept them instead of fighting against the current you will move right along with it.

The Stoics believed that this irresistible flow was simply how fate worked. We may not always understand the flow of our destiny but the more we struggle against it, the worse it will be. This was what the Stoic philosopher Epictetus believed and his life seemed to be a testament of that fact.

He was born a slave, and endured hardship as a young man. He did not struggle against the hand that fate had dealt him however, and simply did the best with what he had. And by the time his freedom was gained he was ready to excel beyond anyone's expectations.

Find Virtue in Pain and Sickness

This one is perhaps hard for many to understand. How in the world could you find anything virtuous about being sick or in pain? But for the Stoic, being able to "grin and bear it" when facing hardship, meant everything in the world. No one says that you will be able to magically get rid of your pain or sickness, but how you react to it can make things better or make things worse.

If someone is suffering from back pain for example, they can either calmly ride out the discomfort or scream in agony. Either way they will still be in pain, but screaming in agony is hardly going to help anything. The Stoic in such situations tries to practice detachment, and tells themselves that the discomfort they feel is real but it does not embody who they are.

I can think of my own father as a perfect example of this practice at work. My dad valiantly struggled with cancer for ten years before he finally succumbed to the illness. But during that time, he never so much as complained. He faced rigorous rounds of chemo and radiation that caused his hair to fall out and his nails to become brittle, but his chief concern was always for others and not himself.

During his last few days on this Earth in fact, with all of his family gathered around, laying in what would we be his death bed—his chief concern was not for his pain, but for his family. He had advice to give to all of us. I remember him telling me to both get a flu shot and to get new tires for my car. Meanwhile we were all choking back tears knowing that his time was short. Nevertheless, my father's focus was not on his own immediate pains and concerns.

That wasn't who he was. He was a caring and compassionate man, and rather than letting the temporary pain of this life obscure that fact, he let his true nature shine forth.

Having that said, as hard as it might be at first, the next time that you are in pain, try to be Stoic about it, and not let the pain overwhelm you to the extent you forget who you are in the process.

Consider Everything Temporary

Life is short! We hear people make that remark all the time, but we often take for granted how true this statement is. We are only here on this planet for a very brief time in the scheme of things, and realizing this to be the case can do much to help us improve where we place our priorities. When one understands the finite nature of life, they are more apt to spend it wisely.

With the advent of modern medicine and improvements in lifestyle, the average person will only live to see their mid-70s. Many more, won't even see that. And while we live whatever amount of life we are allotted; we have to realize that our material possessions are just as temporary as our finite lifespans.

Stoics realized this, and would often ponder the fact that the only thing that couldn't be taken from them was their own thoughts. It might sound kind of strange at first, but it's the truth. Someone could steal everything you own, but they can't rob you of the thoughts and ideas that you lay claim to in your own mind.

It's debatable how much Stoics believed in the afterlife and what might happen to their consciousness when they shed their physical form. But Stoics agreed that just about every material thing we have while still alive—whether it be our money, our loved ones, or even our own personal health; can be taken from us in an instant.

It is for this reason that the Stoics advised not to get too attached to anything in this world. It doesn't mean that you don't care, and you give all the things of this life a cold shoulder, you just make sure that you understand how temporary all of them are and understand that one day they may be no more.

In order to better strengthen our resolve, Stoics advise frequent contemplation on how temporary everything is. It may seem a bit morose at first, but as you consider the fleeting nature of everyone and everything, imagine specific cherished aspects of your life vanishing before your eyes.

Do you have a good job? Imagine you just got fired. Imagine the devastation and uncertainty you would feel knowing that you would have to find another way to earn end's meat. Do you like your car? Imagine it just blew a head gasket and left you stranded at the side of the road. And the list goes on and on.

In order to maintain a good perspective on what's important in life, every once in a while, take stock of your situation. And consider all of the things you have, and just how temporary they really are.

Be Thankful for What You Have

People often say, "Count your blessings!" The phrase may seem cliché, but the statement is rational enough. And a Stoic would advise much the same thing. Similar to the previous practice in considering how temporary things are, a Stoic would also frequently remind themselves of how blessed they actually were. Taking anything for granted was considered highly unethical from the Stoic perspective.

So instead of pining after things that they didn't have, the Stoics sought to cherish what was currently in their possession. As elaborated earlier in this book, Stoics made it a habit to resist accumulating more stuff than they actually needed. Stoics could not easily be accused of being pack rats, since they kept only what was required and nothing more.

Stoics knew that greedy acquisitions were merely a trap that would ensnare them with unhappiness. So instead of looking for more, they valued what they already had. One easy way to train yourself in this regard is to keep a literal inventory of your things and then consider how much you appreciate them. It may sound a bit silly at first, but this is yet another great Stoic practice that really serves to put things into perspective.

Forgive Others for They Know Not What They Do

As much as we try to see the world in black and white, and label folks as either the good guy or the bad guys—it's usually much more complicated than that. According to Stoicism, those whom we deem to be bad, even those that have outright wronged us, are not inherently evil but simply misguided. They quite literally don't know what they are doing, and if they did, they probably wouldn't be doing it in the first place.

If you think about it. This concept makes a lot of sense. Because besides in the comic books with super villains pledging their allegiance to evil, when was the last time you heard anyone in the real world declaring, "I'm a bad guy! I like to do bad stuff!" Most people tend to justify their actions even when they are obviously in the wrong.

It's for this reason that Stoics take a different stance, and advocate that we have sympathy for those that transgress against us rather than have wrath. So instead of immediately flying into a rage when someone cuts us off in traffic—before reaching to honk the horn, stop to consider a few things first. Consider that perhaps that person was in a hurry, maybe they're running late to work, and maybe they didn't even see you there in the first place.

It wasn't a personal slight—it was just something that happened due to the distracted and worried state that they were in at the time. And unless you yourself are perfect, there are probably instances in which you have unintentionally wronged someone yourself. So live and let live, and be ready to forgive. Because often enough, the person who offended you didn't even know they did in the first place. Forgive them, for they know not what they do.

Chapter 7: Reaping the Benefits of Stoicism

Now that we have discussed at length the precepts and practices of Stoicism, let's explore some concrete ways in which Stoicism might be applied to our everyday lives. After just a general overview of this book I think you might agree that the fundamental benefits of stoicism are rather clear. All the same, we live in a complex world in which many nuances need to be taken into consideration. In this final chapter we will take a closer look at just how the benefits of Stoicism might manifest in one's life.

Greater Accountability for Our Actions

Without a doubt, one of the most powerful benefits of stoicism is its ability for people to take accountability for their actions. And in today's world of incessant blame and victimhood mentality—Stoicism serves to strip away this false veneer and show people that at the end of the day, they are indeed responsible for their actions.

If you do something wrong you can't blame your parents, you can't blame society, and you can't blame your personal circumstances. Stoicism after all is well aware of hardships in life and external forces beyond our control But the Stoic would argue that the one thing that we can control, is our own actions. So, in the mind of the Stoic, anything we do; we are indeed accountable for.

Stoicism helps to bring people out of the self-absorption they are trapped in and teaches them that rather than looking outward for their problems, they need to look inward. Many today, try to negate responsibility for the things they do by blaming others for their behavior. To be sure, there are those who face some real hardship and adversity in life. But for a Stoic it doesn't matter.

Because from the Stoic's perspective adversity is just another word for opportunity. And no matter how many curve balls life may throw you, there is always a way to make the most of it. Yes, you may have been born on the rough side of town, grew up poor and were generally more disadvantaged than most.

But instead of dwelling on these external factors that are out of your control, make the best of the situation and take responsibility for the one thing that is always in your possession—your own actions. Successful people the world over have benefited from this philosophy whether they called themselves a Stoic or not.

Stoicism Helps Shield us from Addiction and Unnecessary Attachment

We all have what the Stoics term "insatiability of desires" if we give in to our impulses. According to Stoicism, desire only leads to mor desire, and the more things we get the more we want. This is in itself, the very nature of addiction. The more you drink, do drugs, gamble—whatever the case may be—the more of it you are going to continue to want further down the road.

These things don't satisfy, and only increase desire for them, leading to addiction. Okay, so what's the Stoic solution to this problem? Stepping back and detaching ourselves from the source. Stoicism advises that we need to keep ourselves from vainly chasing after fulfillment, be happy with what we have, and do not so vigorously cling to our possessions/desires that we become addicted to them.

Because addiction is not only a disease—it's slavery. Seneca described it as thus, "So in all our plans and activities, let us do just what we are accustomed to do when we approach a sidewalk vendor who is selling some merchandise or other: let's see what it will cost to get this thing we have our hearts set on. The thing for which nothing is paid often comes at the highest price. I can show you many things whose pursuit and acquisition has cost us our freedom. We would belong to ourselves if these things did not belong to us."

Here Seneca makes it clear, being addicted to anything takes away our freedom and enslaves us to whatever it is that we are addicted to. Stoicism helps us to avoid the extremes of such external attachment. Everything in moderation is the goal, and Stoicism forges a clear path toward that end.

Stoic Principles Foster Strong Leadership

The philosophy of Stoicism encourages us to take responsibility for our actions and as such, puts us on the path to be the leader of our own destiny. Good leaders are those that are selfless rather than selfish after all, and Stoicism specializes in helping us to take the focus off of ourselves and our own misguided perceptions, and back where it needs to be—on the world and how we can do our part to make it a better place.

While a Stoic acknowledges there are outside forces at work, outside of their control, the Stoic knows that they can by their own effort make the situation as good as it can be. This is why Stoicism is naturally conducive for leadership. Here's an interesting example of that in play—think back to the 1970s when NASA was in the midst of the Apollo space program.

There was an ill-fated mission during this period known as Apollo 13. American astronauts were on their way to the moon when damaged equipment nearly cost all of them their lives. The mission leader was a guy named Jim Lovell. If any astronaut was ever a Stoic, Mr. Lovell certainly was.

Because when he realized that one of the onboard oxygen tanks vital to the mission—vital to their very lives—had blown, he stayed completely calm and in the moment. Even though there was a good chance that he and all his crew would soon die, with their craft a veritable coffin forever listlessly drifting in space—did he panic?

No, he did not. Lovell knew full well the situation they were in, yet he calmly—most would say Stoically—radioed ground control to state the famous words, "Houston we have a problem." He didn't shout, "Oh my God! Houston—we're going to die! What are you going to do?"

Despite the massive external threat that loomed, Lovell merely stated the facts as he saw them, and nothing more. Lovel kept a cool, calm, analytical head, and thanks to his rational disposition he was able to formulate a plan with Mission Control that would enable the Apollo team to cut their losses and come home.

The ingenuity of Lovel and his fellow astronauts has since been widely hailed as one of NASA's greatest success stories. This is a prime example of how a strong leader at the helm can take what was initially an abject failure and turn it into a triumph. This of course is just one example, but it demonstrates perfectly well, how Stoic principles do indeed foster strong leadership.

Reduce Stress with a Stoic Lifestyle

For anyone dealing with a lot of stress, Stoic philosophy is tailor made to relieve it! Stoics realized that much of the stress and anxiety that we experience is due to things that are out of our control. We worry about the past and the future for example, but have no control over either one. Yesterday is gone and we have no control over what the future might hold.

Stoics however, teach how one can take things one day at a time and focus on the present instead of worrying about what's outside of their reach. And this holds true for every externality we may face. Stoicism allows us to let go of our anxiety and instead focus on what is in our power to change in the moment. For those who find themselves becoming overwhelmed by all the what if's in life—this is absolutely crucial for reliving stress.

It's also good to keep a journal. Keeping a journal of your daily life may seem a bit trivial at first glance, but Stoics of all stripes have greatly valued the meditation that can be placed upon routine journal entries. In fact, this was the sole express purpose of Marcus Aurelius' "Meditations." It was his personal journal.

As much as others have benefited from his wise entries, he primarily kept the journal to help himself. He never intended to publish his entries. It was simply a way for him to relieve stress at the time. By journaling his thoughts and feelings, he was able to release any pent-up anxiety he may have felt. And if it was good enough for him, this aspect of the Stoic lifestyle will most certainly be good for you too.

Stoicism Makes us Happy

The impetus that kickstarted many philosophies in the first place, has always been the search for happiness—Stoicism among them. Stoics are especially focused on finding happiness. How? By being happy with what they have. Stoicism tells us that the reason why people are dissatisfied is because they are always looking for fulfillment outside of themselves and then become disappointed when they cannot find it.

The problem with basing your happiness on external factors is just that—*they are external.* This is why Stoicism lets us know that the best way to find happiness is to find it from within. The Stoic therefore is primed to only invest their happiness in things that are well within their control.

For the happiness that a Stoic is directed to find is not one that is fleeting but one that will last. This Stoic happiness, that they call, "eudaimonia" which roughly translates as "the good life." The Stoic take on the good life is not one of excess, but of quite literally living a good, and virtuous life.

Stoics believed that happiness resulted as a natural consequence of being good. When you are helpful to others for example, it just might make you feel good and put a smile on your face. If you talk to anyone who regularly volunteers their time in service for others, they will tell you the most rewarding thing about it is the happiness that they feel from serving a greater good.

Stoic Virtue Prevents Snap Judgment

We live in a judgmental world and many of us are used to making snap judgments at a moment's notice. In some regard, this is only natural. As a part of human development along the way, we have learned to jump to quick conclusions out of a necessity for our survival in a dangerous and uncertain world.

If for example, you were walking down a dark alley and see a large hulking figure walking toward you with a knife. In this circumstance most would forgive you for tensing up, and making a snap judgment that your life might be in danger. But other than in extreme situations, the judgments we make are often far from accurate.

And in the world of social media in which every aspect of our lives is often on display, the propensity for glaring misjudgment is so profound, it is appalling. Stoicism helps us to slow down and consider the situation very carefully before we start judging. This can be useful in a wide variety of situations and settings in life.

It's an active process however, so if you find yourself tempted to make a snap judgement against someone or something, pause your thought processes for a moment and remind yourself that you don't might not know all the facts. If you can actively disrupt judgmental thoughts as soon as they occur, you will soon cease to have them altogether.

This Stoic method has actually been so effective that it's been picked up and used in what we now call "Cognitive Behavioral Therapy" (CBT). As we will discuss later in this book, this so-called modern therapy is really only different from Stoicism in name. Because CBT, just like Stoicism, asks you to step back from your preconceived notions and see the world as it really is.

It's Good for Our Physical and Mental Well Being

We live in a world of high anxiety, and it's easy to get overwhelmed. Stoicism however, allows us to step back from what we are doing and take a deep breath.

Stoics knew that the true source of anxiety was in worrying over things that they could not control. People worried about what others thought, they worried about what might happen in the future, and a whole host of other things that were beyond their direct control.

The Stoics therefore taught that it was necessary to let go of these things we could not change and instead take liberty in the things that we could. It is a very freeing experience. Stoics also value moderation in food, drink, and all other things that could be done in excess. This in turn leads to a healthier physical lifestyle. As it turns out, a little bit of Stoicism, just like moderation, is good for both body and mind.

Stoicism Eases the Fear of Death

Stoicism tackles perhaps the greatest fear of all in its efforts to unmask death. Stoics teach us that death is nothing to fear, it is simply a natural process.

Stoics realized that the reason why people feared death so much, was because it presented itself as a complete unknown. But Stoicism allows one to rationalize what death really is and thereby take the sting right out of it.

As of the writing of this book, much of the world is in the grip of the pandemic outbreak known as the Coronavirus.

History will record how much various populaces panicked during this epidemic, and how many looked at the threat with a calm resolve.

We will remember how many cast a suspicious eye toward their neighbor and how many extended a hand to help. Stoicism does not encourage anyone to be needlessly reckless, but it also firmly advocates courage, even in the face of death.

The Stoic Mindset Gives Us Good Perspective

One of the best benefits about the Stoic mindset is that it gives us good perspective on life. Sometimes we can become so self-absorbed that we feel the whole world revolves around us. Stoicism however, serves to remind one of how insignificant they really are! The idea might sound like a negative one at first, but upon closer examination its actually quite freeing.

Just think about it. Half the time we think things are important, when they are really not important at all. And other times we fret and worry about stuff that we have no business worrying about in the first place. There are all kinds of trivial circumstance that we can obsess over, but in the grand scheme of things many of them really don't matter at all.

Let's say it's announced that you're getting a new supervisor on your job. You don't know anything about this person, yet you spend the whole week worrying about what kind of person they are, if they are going to drastically change work protocol, and whether or not they are going to like you. This is completely useless.

You can't control who the company hires, and even if there are some changes in store, the best you can do is roll with the punches.

And that goes for any situation in life, there's no guarantee that there might not be hardship in the short term, but the level of importance we place on situations is usually far greater than we merit. And as soon as we realize it's not nearly as big of a deal as we make it—we can breathe a huge sigh of relief as a result. The Stoic mindset helps to keep these things in perspective.

Stoicism Gets us Better in Tune with Our Emotions

If someone hears the word Stoic, they usually think of someone or something that is devoid of emotion. But on the contrary, stoicism actually helps to get better in tune with your emotions. It was not the goal of the Stoics to get rid of emotion, they just wanted to get rid of irrational inflamed passion that led to distress and discord.

This is because Stoicism helps us to realize when an emotional reaction is valid and when it is not. When we have an emotional reaction, it is because we are agreeing to be provoked by something. Whether that reaction be a pleasant or an unpleasant one, we are the ones allowing it to transpire. The Stoics sought to prevent such inflamed passion from overriding their sense of reason.

Often enough people act and do things in the moment that are not only contrary to their best interests but contrary to their own emotions. Just imagine the quarrelling couple who love each other dealing. The real emotion they feel for each other is love and affection. But trivial arguments have led them to give in to darker impulses of anger and rage, belying the true emotional attachment that they feel for each other.

This is why even a loved one if driven into passionate excess enough, could slam a door in your face and scream that they "hate you" when in reality this is far from the case. This example is maybe a little extreme, but we see similar things all the time. We speak of how people sometimes say things they don't really mean because they were "caught up in the moment." But this is exactly what the Stoics seek to avoid. They do not want to be caught up in the brief moment of inflamed passion, and thereby negate the true intentions of their heart. It is in this fashion that the Stoics enabled themselves to stay focused on what really mattered to them, and get in rightful tune with their emotions as a result.

It is for this reason that it is important once again to press the pause button when you feel that you are on the verge of being overwhelmed by emotion. Many of us can feel that upswell of emotional angst as it happens, and if you train ourselves well enough, we can disrupt it and replace it with rational thought. Stoicism helps us to do just that.

Staying Grounded with a Stoic Mindset

Fine tuning your finite existence on this planet requires being able to maximize what's most important. By important, we are referring to the fundamental qualities of who you are as a person. Stoicism helps you to reset the clock and get back to square one. It helps you to realize what you have and what you can do with it.

You have all of the tools in your own personal tool box that you need. You just have to make use of them. And if something happens to be outside of your power for change, the Stoic mindset allows you to cut your losses and move on to bigger and better things.

If you can learn to be the master of your own willpower, your destiny is in your hands. Simply by remembering that you are the captain of your own ship, will help you stay grounded and balanced even in the worst of life's storms.

Stoicism can Make Lemonade out of Life's Lemons

There's an old saying, "If life gives you lemons, make lemonade." This is perhaps one of the most Stoic expressions ever made.

Because for a Stoic, one of the most important things you could learn is to make the best out of bad situations.

During the hardships of life, instead of wallowing in your own sorrow, take the Stoic principle of perseverance to pull yourself back up onto your feet.

Take for example the case of someone who has just gone through a divorce. Such a sudden separation can be devastating and traumatic, but the only path forward is—well, you guessed it—forward! As hard as it may be, you have to move on and make the best of it. This means not dwelling on the past and what you could have done better, but instead focusing on what it is you can do now.

Adopt the Stoic virtue of courage so that you can face this lemon life has dealt you, as an opportunity rather than a setback. For even in what at first appears to be the most negative of circumstances, you can always find a positive. If for example, your spouse was controlling and constantly dictating everything you did, the possibility of being free from their grasp could open new doors for you. Being on your own has suddenly vested you with a newfound freedom you did not have before. Embrace it. Use it as an excuse to go to all of those places you always wanted to go. See all of those people that you always wanted to see. And stay out as late as you want, with no repercussions. This of course is just one hypothetical example among many, but yes, whatever lemon life might throw, gird yourself to face it with courage and adventure rather than agony and despair.

I know sometimes such things can seem to be much easier said than done, but in the end, you really have only two choices. You could remain miserable and stuck in the past, or you can kick it into high gear and forge your own new and exciting future. It's all completely up to you. You are the writer of your own destiny—so keep your life's narrative as interesting as possible!

Stoicism Helps to Foster Greater Acceptance

Domineering people who seek to curb the actions and opinions of others, are some of the most unhappy and unfulfilled individuals you could ever meet. Because no matter how tyrannical one's disposition, there will always be external forces that remain firmly outside of their personal jurisdiction.

By contrast, the more one accepts this fact, the more accepting they are of other people as a consequence. The Stoic could be in the room with any given number of people with any given number of opinions and beliefs, and get along with all of them just fine. Just because someone doesn't agree with you, doesn't mean you need to argue with them, or shut them out.

The Stoic intuitively knows to value the differences among people even if it's not something that they themselves personally buy into. A Stoic could be a lone conservative in the midst of a bunch of liberals for example, and it wouldn't matter in the least. For a Stoic, a mere difference in opinion would not render any verdict on how they value an individual.

In the toxic political environment of today, it would do all of us some good to take on the example of such Stoic tolerance. Political polarization would be a thing of the past if we would simply learn to respect differences in opinion. And if you apply the principles of stoicism to your life, it will indeed foster greater acceptance of others as a result. And you will find yourself all the happier for it.

Chapter 8: The Rise of Modern Stoicism

The movement now known as modern Stoicism began in the late 20th Century. Modern Stoicism differs from classical Stoicism in that Modern Stoics follow the principles of Stoicism from a purely secular sense. As mentioned earlier in this book, ancient Stoics viewed the divine power of the universe as the Logos that permeates all creation. Modern Stoics do not get that deep into such big, metaphysical concepts such as fate and the divine will of the universe.

Instead Modern Stoics tend to focus on simply how to live a better life down here on Earth. Stoicism has always been practical for everyday life, but Modern Stoics have broken down the precepts even further so that they are even more effective for modern living. Here in this chapter we will examine how Stoicism has had a resurgence in modern life.

Modern Stoicism in Philosophy

Stoicism, received various starts and stops throughout the centuries with philosophical thinkers as diverse as Montaigne, Descartes, and even Teddy Roosevelt, all signing on to draw their own interpretations from time to time.

But these brief moments of insight into the past did not constitute a movement. It wasn't until the late 20th century that a new push toward Modern Stoicism truly began.

In many ways it was thanks to the development of the internet that not only was Stoicism brought to new wide-ranging audiences, but also the fact that the web allowed these newfound Stoics to connect to each other from all over the world. Soon new groups were put together on online platforms such as Reddit and Facebook, that allowed Modern Stoics to hash out their views on Stoic philosophy.

But most importantly was the birth of the so-called "New Stoa," a philosophical collective designed to mainstream the Modern Stoic mindset to the masses. Formed as the "Stoic Registry" in 1996, it has since served as a resource for budding Stoics all over the globe. From here, the movement steadily grew and several more online groups were formed while several books on the subject of Modern Stoicism began to make the rounds.

Most notable in these efforts are the likes of Ryan Holiday and John Sellars. Holiday is a California born, millennial media mogul, turned modern Stoic famous for his ability to explain complex philosophy in an easy to understand manner. John Sellars meanwhile is an esteemed philosophy professor. The backgrounds of these two modern sages are quite different, but their message is the same. Stoicism works, and it can be applied to modern life.

Sellars in particular, is also among the founders of "Stoic Week" which challenges people from all over the world to take part in a challenge to adopt Stoic practices for 7 days straight. The project began as a standalone event, but has since continued on a regular basis with thousands signing up for the challenge.

Even before Holiday or Sellars' books began making the rounds however, there was one niche group in which a brand of Modern Stoicism was already flourishing—the U.S. Military. James Stockdale in particular, is well known for pushing forward a more modern approach to Stoic philosophy.

Stockdale as a Navy Veteran who served in Vietnam, found solace in the work of Epictetus, the Stoic who was born a slave and embraced Stoic philosophy to make sense of the hardship of life. During his time in Vietnam, James was captured and made a prisoner of war, it was the Stoic principles of courage and endurance that helped him to make it through.

Modern Stoicism in Psychology

Psychology does in deed owe a lot to Stoicism.

The very word is derived from the Greek term "psyche" which for the ancient Stoics meant the seat of emotion, consciousness, or for lack of a better term—the "soul."

But pushing aside the more metaphysical interpretations, the idea of psyche in Psychology does indeed encompass what we have come to understand as human consciousness. For modern psychologists, the psyche represents both the conscious and unconscious mind, as well as a person's emotional states.

This is all common parlance and can be traced right back to the days of Socrates, Zeno, and the like. But the field in which Modern Stoicism has really taken hold, when it comes to psychology, is in the practice of Cognitive Behavioral Therapy (CBT). Cognitive Behavioral Therapy literally seeks to teach the patient how to change their mind—*how to change the way they think.*

This is done in an incremental pattern to change thoughts and behaviors. If for example, someone who is suffering from social anxiety is afraid to go to public places, CBT will create comprehensive exercises for them to embrace the Stoic virtue of courage.

A big part of this involves the "negative visualization" that we discussed earlier in this chapter. The patient will often be told to keep a journal and just before they are getting ready to confront something that makes them anxious—such as going out in public—they will envision all the things they think could go wrong and write down all of these negative thoughts in the journal.

Usually the patient finds that things did not turn out as bad as they thought, and even if they did, their journaling helps them to critique the event in a rational manner so that they can adjust their behavior in a manner that will lead to more successful engagements in the future. Along with combatting phobias and anxieties, Cognitive Behavioral Therapy is also good for helping patients gain control of negative impulses. Impulse control of course, is a basic tenant of Stoicism.

For someone who has anger management issues for example, and trouble controlling their impulses, CBT can use the Stoic notion of teaching the individual to look toward the long term good rather than the short-term gain. If someone feels compelled to lash out at drivers who cut them off in traffic for example, CBT helps the individual to take a breath and think of the long-term consequences that would happen if an ugly incident of road rage should erupt.

Practicing CBT enables the participant to visualize what might happen should they lose control.

They could get into a fight with another motorist, get arrested, and go to jail, among other things. By considering these scenarios in advance with CBT, the participant can learn to change their behavior should the occasion arrive.

Instead of succumbing to their impulses, they can now step back and better analyze the situation. This is of course, standard Stoic practice at work. From Chrysippus to Seneca, the rational reasoning of the Stoic has sought to blunt the passions and bring forth rational analysis. And so too does Cognitive Behavioral Therapy.

Another area in which some aspects of Stoicism are used in psychological treatment is in the field of "positive psychology." Positive Psychology revolves around the individual "character strengths" of a person, and seeks to channel them in a constructive manner that brings out the best in someone. This too can be likened to Stoicism and its focus on obtaining virtue in life.

Modern Stoicism as a Political Movement

Ancient Stoicism was not too invested in the political environment of their day, in fact when Zeno was asked by the Macedonian King Anitgonus Gonatas to come to his Kingdom as an adviser, Zeno refused, only agreeing to send one of his students instead. From the beginning, Stoics were mostly apolitical, and when the political structure of the day sought to make them partisans, they avoided it.

It was Plato—not Zeno—after all, who wrote "The Republic" and advised that philosopher kings would be best to rule society. The Stoics on the other hand, would for the most part, have nothing of the sort. Marcus Aurelius was perhaps the only real exception to this rule. But even in his case, he was not someone naturally seeking political power, so much as it sought him.

At any rate, today there is a growing movement for Stoicism in the modern political arena. In many ways the current political climate in the world—and most especially the United States—is one of volatility. What could Stoic principles do to heal the political divide? Many are indeed looking toward Stoicism as a possible solution to heal our political wounds.

Stoicism allows us to rationally look at all sides of an argument. And instead of talking over one another, the Stoic is equipped to listen alternative points of view and accept the ideas of others, even if they themselves do not necessarily agree. As all of these trends seem to suggest, whether it's philosophy, psychology, or politics—Modern Stoicism is on the rise.

Conclusion: The Stoic State of Mind

In many ways, being a Stoic is not so much a practice as it is a state of mind. The Stoic seeks to keep everything in the right perspective, in order to make the best of their circumstances. As testament to this mindset at work, you can could take two people—a Stoic and non-Stoic—and put them in the same situation, and yet have two completely different reactions.

Let's say that the Stoic and his non-Stoic buddy are driving out in the middle of nowhere when their car runs out of gas. The non-Stoic looking around at the desolate countryside might gasp, "Oh no! We're stuck out here!" The Stoic meanwhile would look around at the scenery, feel the cool breeze blowing by, and the sun shining down, and say, "Well—it looks like a good day for a walk!"

Faced with such a choice, that old phrase, "grin and bear it" comes to mind. It's not to say that walking for a mile with a gas can isn't a hardship, it's just an acknowledgment that resistance will only make matters worse. If you run out of gas, sitting on the side of the road and crying about it won't help matters one bit.

From the Stoic perspective, we need to take whatever cards we are dealt and play them to the best of our ability. If that means using our feet to walk to a gas station so be it. We need to make the best of things in this life.

It's not always easy to just suck it up and move forward but as the precepts in this book have shown, there is indeed a way to get through most situations if we have the right attitude and mindset.

So, if you find yourself struggling to get by in life, overwhelmed by disappointment and failure, don't dwell on your setbacks. Just cut your losses and move forward to the best of your ability. There's no sense in beating yourself up over the past—what's done is done. Your vision has been clouded by regret and second-guesses for far too long. Put those things of the past to the side.

Now's your time to move forward. You don't have to sit on the side lines bemoaning your circumstances any longer. Now's your time to take advantage of the best that life has to offer. Now's the time to fully develop a Stoic state of mind.

Thank you for reading, and good luck!

Made in the USA
Monee, IL
20 November 2022

18214725R00085